Our Choice
Extinction or Evolution

• • •

Our Choice
Extinction or Evolution

The Analyst and The Astrologer

Richard Spitzer and Linda Schurman

**Choices for our Future Economic, Technological,
Environmental, and Social Survival**

ISBN: 1513626272
ISBN 13: 9781513626277
Library of Congress Control Number: 2017916046
Soothe Script Publishing LLC, Ithaca, New York

Table of Contents

Introduction

● ● ●

Where on Earth Are We Going?

*"A pessimist sees the difficulty in every opportunity;
an optimist sees the opportunity in every difficulty."*

WINSTON CHURCHILL

Whether we choose to face it or avoid it, chaos and confusion are spreading across the globe like a hurricane, washing over the lives of the nearly eight billion people who live here. Emergencies are rising before our eyes in the form of climate catastrophes, financial and economic disruption, civil revolutions and wars, and mass migrations of people to escape their native habitats not seen since the end of World War II. Simultaneously, amid all the global chaos, Wall Street's financial experts are celebrating what they interpret as the most prosperous economy in this century!

Whole populations are having an "identity crisis" as these displaced people have left their cultural supports behind and nations who are receiving them feel threatened. Economic prosperity is dwindling for all except the richest people throughout the globe. Under these conditions, people often deny that what is happening to them is really taking place, preferring to think that things will return to the familiar – a phenomenon referred to as "normalcy bias." This thinking can have severe consequences. When people do not face the facts of an imminent disaster such as a financial or environmental crisis or act to protect their loved ones, the negative effect that the disaster has upon them is much greater.

Ancient human tendencies that point to ethnic and racial minorities for our discontent are rising as the "blame game" is once again inserting itself into our public discourse. The re-emergence of white supremacists and neo-Nazis in America is illustrative of historic hatreds that have been with us for centuries. Dark conspiracy theories are swirling around us that we are being spied upon by our enemies, or the "police state," or the very institutions we helped to build - to the point that we trust no one.

Recent history has presented us with many highly visible sources in the main stream media who put corporate interests, profits, and ratings before their responsibility to investigate and report the truth. This leads us in the direction of "buying the story" of the loudest, most negative, least credible, least scientific, and least informed individuals who become a "mouthpiece" for our collective anger.

Fear of the unknown or unfamiliar resides at the bottom of our collective psyche and many people feel either uprooted or invaded. Massive techno-logical change, so-called global trade, the elimination of entire sectors of the job market, the massive economic control and manipulation of giant trans-national banks and corporations all have played a part in removing our sense of being in charge of our lives, our historic belief that we have options and opportunities, and our long-cherished ideal of freedom to choose our fates. Human-induced global climate change combined with nuclear and chemical pollution is such a huge "elephant in the room" as to be incomprehensible for the human species that is used to devising close-at-hand local solutions to problems and often feels powerless to change the larger tide of events.

What does it all mean - Doom or Bloom?

In *The Guardian* (Dec 1, 2016), British theoretical physicist, Stephen Hawking, states: "We face awesome environmental challenges: climate change, food production, overpopulation, the decimation of other species, epidemic disease, and acidification of the oceans. Together, they are a reminder that we are at the most dangerous moment in the development of humanity. We now have the technology to destroy the planet on which we live, but have not developed the ability to escape it."

We, as human beings, are now faced with choices our ancestors never encountered. There have always been threats, but for the first time in history the challenges we face can result in irreversible and undesirable outcomes. Yet, every one of today's challenges and opportunities are the result of choices that we made or let someone else make for us. Albert Einstein is famously credited by many as saying: "The definition of insanity is doing something over and over and expecting a different result." We would suggest that much too frequently, unreliable information is dispensed in the public arena about what is happening and what should be done.

There are many people who have nearly given up hope that humanity has the inclination and/or capability to save itself along with most life on earth. Some environmental scientists are observing that we may be moving toward a mass decimation of life here on earth not seen since the great Permian Extinction which occurred 250 million years ago. We are not among these people. Our point of view is concerned with shedding light on contexts that will lead to making choices that will serve the greater good and are in alignment with current conditions.

The purpose of this book is to present the challenges that we absolutely must face along with ideas and solutions, many of which are already being quietly implemented all over the world, as we speak. Throughout history people have had great insights that have come to them virtually "out of the blue", and that have set humanity on a course never imagined. With open minds and hearts and a willingness to work together, this kind of inspiration and innovation may arise again to save us.

"Choose to be optimistic, it feels better."

DALAI LAMA XIV

As Futurists, we are using integrative techniques involving modern data analysis, information theory involving trends, and astrological patterns that have served humanity for more than 5,000 years. The numerous and critical issues facing humanity and the planet are interrelated. Thus, the foundational issue of this book is the economics that drive most of the life-support issues of the modern world.

We will survey the six most critical issues that contain both natural components and human intervention. They are: 1) Economics; 2) Information; 3) Technology; 4) Energy; 5) the Environment; and 6) Human consciousness change, philosophical and societal transformations. Our view is that we are literally in an intense battle between "nature" and "human nature."

We also can see beyond the present horizon of time to some impressive and grand solutions to both the present ongoing global emergencies and what the future may hold concerning the re-imagining of human civilization. Fresh data and planetary patterns that lie ahead suggest the possibility of new and innovative ideas that support a rebirth of the human presence - one that lives in concert with life on earth and in cooperation with one another. To many, this would seem hopelessly idealistic. To us, no less than this is acceptable. Doom is not acceptable for our children or grandchildren as they grow and bloom before our eyes trusting us to reverse the swirling landscapes of lifeless dust into fields of flowers.

> *"We are apt to shut our eyes against a painful truth...*
> *For my part, I am willing to know the whole truth;*
> *to know the worst; and to provide for it."*
>
> PATRICK HENRY

Chapter 1

●　●　●

A New Collaboration to Deciphering the Future

This book contains a merger of two disciplines, Astrology and Data Macro-Analysis, both of which recognize and work within the influence of cycles. It describes critical factors affecting our survival, visible and invisible; natural and human induced; multiple viewpoints on the issues; and costs to the public at large. We will present our information from each of our own disciplines, integrate our information, and speak from our own personal experiences and expertise.

This collaborative approach includes the understanding of what astrology brings to us all. As an astrologer, Linda Schurman observes and studies the astronomical planetary patterns that have occurred during events of historical significance, including the rise and fall of major civilizations in the past, great discoveries and inventions, and what relevant information they have for us now as many of these placements are reoccurring today and into the future. Since most people are unfamiliar with astrological references, Linda keeps them to a minimum, with charts and planetary placements located at the end of the book. She refers to information from scientists, economists, and political analysts who are publishing what she sees are in alignment with planetary pictures, "connecting the dots" from the cosmos to our lives here on earth. In her online newsletters (The SootheSayer.com), radio interviews, and previous books: *What Next?: A*

Survival Guide to the 21ˢᵗ Century (2007), and *Fast Forward: Surviving the Race to the Future* (2012), Linda has predicted how the period we are in now (2008–2024) simulates the Great Depression of the 1930s, with the rise of Fascism in Europe, World War II, the development of nuclear power, and, going into the 2020s, the American Revolution, the French Revolution, and the Industrial Revolution. History does not exactly repeat itself but it "rhymes."

As a modern data analyst, Richard Spitzer has noted many similar unfolding patterns in macro-economics, patterns of investment, and cycles of prosperity vs. cycles of economic decline. For many years, he has been an executive in both global business firms and research consultancies. He has been an advisor to corporate and banking industries with respect to consumer markets, business trends, communications effectiveness, and long-range planning about future risks and opportunities in business, technology, and social conditions. Over the past 12 years, Richard has developed and operated a business based upon a new "predictive analytics" methodology for macroeconomic trends. He continues today within the context of his own consulting work. Currently, he is observing data that sets off alarms for him as to the economic future of humanity.

We have written this book with a common goal and shared concerns, but we still want to offer the maximum breadth of ideas and possibilities. Thus, each chapter is in two parts:

1. Richard writes in the macro-level view of trends, challenges, and future opportunities.
2. Linda writes from the astrological perspective, about historical cycles, the relevance to today, and specific actions take meet the current challenges.

Each respective section of the chapter is identified as written by The Analyst (Richard) or The Astrologer (Linda).

Both authors realize the numerous and critical issues facing humanity and understand that most are interrelated. Both know that there are no "absolutes." The broadly accepted beliefs about reality through the ages change as more information reveals itself and becomes available. Even science has altered its assessments of reality multiple times. Einstein's physics subsumed Newton's. The discovery of "dark matter and dark energy" has turned our realities upside down as have formulations like Chaos Theory, the discovery and proof of the "God Particle," and the recent evidence supporting the Theory of Entanglement. Economic and financial cycles frequently repeat themselves, but new contexts and innovative ideas and decisions can alter them.

The authors know we cannot fix everything at once, but metaphorically, we must "stop the bleeding before we can make the repair." Both have also accessed information about people throughout the world who are presenting both technological and societal solutions to these challenges and implementing them. Both will present points of view coming from their contrasting disciplines, the latest information supporting their insights, and possible trajectories into the future.

What is important to the authors of this book is that people understand the most critical issues of our time and that we all have decisions to make. We can ignore them, deny that they exist, or step up to the plate and confront the challenges and the people who are in positions of power and responsibility to make things right.

The Choice is Ours!

Chapter 2

● ● ●

Our Approach: The Challenges, Trends, Cycles and Choices

❖ The Analyst

> *"You read a book from beginning to end.*
> *You run a business the opposite way.*
> *You start with the end, then you do*
> *everything you must to reach it."*

HAROLD GENEEN

We all have a new job to do - to identify the serious challenges to our survival, improve life for the "greater good," determine how to stop the current trends, and work at it every day. The proposition of our book is simple — we need a new approach to resolve our problems since the mindset and methods of the past will not work adequately or in time.

Together we will be answering these questions:

*   **What do we need do first?**
*   **What tools and methods are available?**
*   **What can we learn from the past?**
*   **What might be available in the future?**

In this chapter we explain the how, why, and benefits of the merger of two analytic disciplines as the basis for our observations, recommendations, and forecasts.

There are plenty of books, forecasters, think tanks, and business, scientific, political, and economic leaders with proposals for dealing with our immediate challenges. This book is not a critique of their proposals, but an alternative approach that does not rely solely on the very same processes of planning, decision-making, and actions that got us into this mess.

What are the Extinction/Evolution Challenges?

We use a common set of principles with several criteria for identifying each survival challenge:

*   Based largely on economics and/or ideology, not the ultimate greater good for all people.
*   Part of high-profile, high-visibility news on a continuous basis.
*   Elicits multiple points of view, controversy, and constituencies.
*   Needed solutions that are complex, costly, will take the time to fix, and need immediate action.
*   Subject to patterns and cycles that have both natural/astrological relationships and human intervention influences.

We are literally in an intense battle between "nature" and "human nature."

People are mostly optimistic but cautious by nature. However, our natural instincts have been overwhelmed with the speed, volume, diversity, and contradiction of information and the behavior of our institutions. The most recent and disturbing evidence happened in the 2016 election — the promotion and accommodation, by too many people, of "fake news."

We have many challenges that need our attention and each is a priority to some proponent. There are constituencies for every belief and ideology. Every day we can find headlines that represent many of the evolution/extinction issues. You may not agree completely with our list but they do represent pervasive global threats.

Many issues are critical, but we need a definite place to start and set the priorities based on the highest-level types of decision-choices model. We've designated the following six issues as the most influential choice challenges.

The six issues in our order of immediate challenges include the following:

1. Economic-based norms and ideology have consequences for virtually every aspect of global survival today - from income disparity to the fragile and once again irrational exuberance in the markets.
2. The information revolution has overloaded us with news, forecasts, and opinions, and it is out of control. Too often, information is no longer the proverbial knowledge but elegant hi-tech propaganda.
3. Technology is both a solution and an accomplice to our threats. We need to focus technological investment and priorities on practical reality.
4. Energy is the literal fuel of global economics and politics.
5. Environmental threats are real and can be observed; denial does not work.
6. Social, cultural, and religious stresses are at a high-level today and the conflicts hamper efforts on other critical issues.

Our book will not leave you in doubt about our views and concerns. We believe the threats are real and the consequences may be irreversible. Our goal is to reawaken awareness of the issues and suggest how to find solutions.

We present the extinction/evolution issues in the context of several themes:

* **Choices made "for the greater good"** of all people and the preservation of our planet. We all must make choices, from the individual level to global leadership. But the evidence so far is that most choices are not for the common good, but ignite or aggravate real survival threats.

* There are two core and connected threats and a contemporary word will get everyone's attention — **"terrorism."** For our work here, the two challenges are **"Economic terrorism" and "Information terrorism."**

While current political and physical terrorism are certainly gruesome and we need to address the origins and seek resolutions, there are other forms of terrorism that affect millions, billions, of people every day.

* The most significant obstacles to the "greater good" are the choices made by the few for their economic gain and power. Their choices will eventually reduce or destroy the very sources of their wealth and power – growing, prosperous populations and a productive planet. **This is economic terrorism**.

* The second component – **information terrorism** – is the intensity of incomplete, often intentionally false and self-serving information and news to manipulate political, economic, and social interests. You may know the quote by Francis Bacon: "Knowledge itself is power" (*"Meditationes Sacrae,"* 1597). Absolute practical knowledge is no longer the only source of power. Knowledge has been

supplanted by views and opinions as an extremely high-level form of propaganda that is subject to little control socially or legally.

Everything is connected to everything else.

"There is a proper dignity and proportion to every act of life."

MARCUS AURELIUS

There is no isolated single solution anymore. Every aspect of civilization is intricately linked to one another, so we are attempting to set priorities with the six challenges.   Every economic issue affects the state of healthcare, quality of air and water, affordability of a house, jobs, and living a safe and secure life. Every energy decision is also an economic decision, an environmental impact issue, and a job creation opportunity. We have summarized our key extinction/evolution issues and their connections to the most immediate consequences.

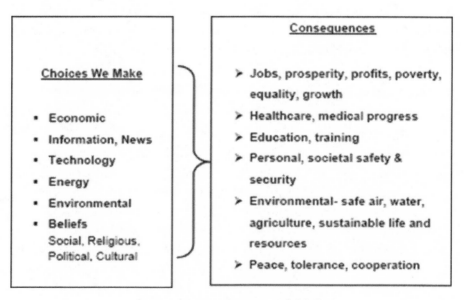

Source: 3iconexxion research LLC.

Despite the threats, there is still time and there are opportunities to make changes that will make a difference globally and at the individual level. The critical time cycles we are concerned about started with a vengeance in 2000 and the Internet bubble crash, with 2008 the last epic example of a world out-of-sync. The 2016 election was possibly the final call for our attention. And now these challenges will be the central issues over the next three presidential cycles, for 12 years. It will be the decisive time for us to make the choice for a change in politics or a continuation of the present trends.

> *"Those who cannot remember the past*
> *are condemned to repeat it."*

GEORGE SANTAYANA

The ways in which we make choices and decisions are no longer adequate for the complexity and needs we have created.

Modern decision makers use an extensive array of information collected since the start of the Industrial Revolution. We have ignored an even more established source of guidance that served humanity well for thousands of years, well in the context of the ways in which humans made choices that enabled us to survive until this day. Since we are now threatened with way-of-life issues and current decision norms are not working so well, it is time to reconsider the mechanisms that seem to be part of our decision-making DNA. Today's complexity requires the integration of disciplines that connect the contexts of challenges and opportunities in ways not done before.

To get right to the point: there is a universal construct that is reflected in all that we do, which has been neglected as an explanatory variable. The relationship of astronomical movements to our observable human behavior have been systematically observed, organized, and documented by the art and science of astrology.

The combination of astrology and modern macro-analytics might seem like an odd pairing, but that is exactly the point. Conventional methods of analysis and guidance are failing us and we can't rely only on old methods to find new solutions. A blending of ancient practices and modern analytic theories will provide a more encompassing context for how the forces outside of our control interact with real-life human interventions.

If you are skeptical of astrology, do not give up on this book yet. If we've been making choices throughout history and have arrived at a point of potential extinction, we propose it is time to think about what we have been doing wrong and seek other mechanisms to change the course that we are on. Humans have evolved far beyond being tied to natural cycles that dominated life for thousands of years. We have evolved intellectually and technologically, and believe we can make choices that we can control.

So, for now, please accept the premise that astrology represents a way to identify external forces that have potential influences on our thinking and behavior. The best outcomes will be those decisions made when best aligned with natural influences rather than against or out of sync with them.

Astrological history documents the cycles of social, political, economic and other changes involving human decisions and behavior. Of course, most cycles are only evident when looking back, because that is the nature of history. But we now have data analysis technology to adapt astrological history to modern trends and macro-analysis.

This book is also not just our personal opinions; it is based on evidence from our respective disciplines. At the simplest level, identifying the most important and persistent threats is as easy as reading the news headlines every day.

Astrological and macro-trend analyses connect to the very same issues we are discussing. Over the past 50 years Richard has been involved in hundreds of studies about business, economic and social conditions, trends, and future opportunities. Linda has have been writing about astrological patterns, historical and contemporary, for more than 40 years.

Public information and news is familiar to more people than astrology and is also a very useful trend research tool. Over time, if an issue is continuing to be covered in the news, and especially if it is increasing, it is because the issue has enough substance, interest, new relevant data, and apparent credibility to warrant being "newsworthy." News in its broadest sense reports on what we are thinking and talking about and doing or not doing. This is just one aspect of our macro-analyses which covers both historical astrological patterns and what we have measured and recorded with traditional methods for the past 150+ years.

We make our case for the influence of cycles on our choices and in our lives because recognizing and using neglected cyclical influences must be integrated into our normal way of making choices.

Cycles are identifiable patterns that occur repeatedly over time on a scale that can be measured and have sufficient history to observe the consistency of the cycles. Cycles can vary in duration, range, and level of influence, but must have similar characteristics present in each repetition.

"Cycles" are extensively documented, measured, and accepted in every aspect of life.

The natural world's influences are cyclical and a permanent part of our everyday life, from human biology to electromagnetism to planetary cycles. The natural cycles represent macro-influences that we generally cannot change, but often fail to accommodate in today's challenges. We have learned to accommodate or moderate or even harness some of nature's cycles, in agriculture to human health to technology, but we typically ignore or reject the very same universal influences on the newer disciplines of economics and politics.

All cycles have the same profile. Does this look familiar?

Every cycle has the same basic repeating pattern or shape. Here is a standard picture of a radio signal.

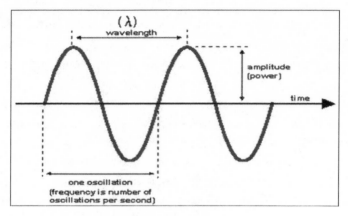

Source: Wikipedia

Go to *Wikipedia* and you can finds hundreds of definitions of established cycles. This is an abbreviated list that demonstrates the cyclical nature of everything.

* Time and calendar cycles
* Planetary cycles
    * Astronomical cycles
    * Climate and weather cycles
    * Geological cycles
* Organic cycles
    * Agricultural cycles
    * Biological and medical cycles
    * Brain waves and cycles
* Physics cycles
    * Mathematics of waves and cycles
    * Electromagnetic spectrum
    * Sound waves

* Miscellaneous cycles
    * Economic and business cycles
    * Music and rhythm cycles
    * Religious, mythological, and spiritual cycles
    * Social and cultural cycles
    * Military and war
    * Literature

If we accept that cycles exist in virtually everything we encounter, we must also recognize that cycles have conditions, catalysts, results, and consequences. The better we can recognize a cycle we are in and anticipate the next one, the better we can plan our actions within the nature of that cycle.

If you could remove the labeling from each chart, you would have a tough time distinguishing solar flare cycles from economic cycles.

There are no disputes about solar cycles. These cycles are part of the natural world.

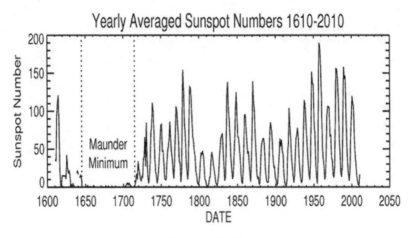

Source: NASA

There are no doubts about business cycles and the key evidence-employment.

What influences business cycles and the economic choices that influence economic activity?

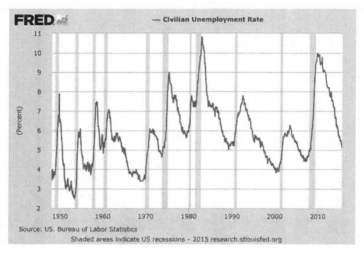

Source : FRED

There are no debates about brain wave activities - this is our brainwave activity and it is defined by cycles.

Issue: What influences our ideas, thought and decisions?

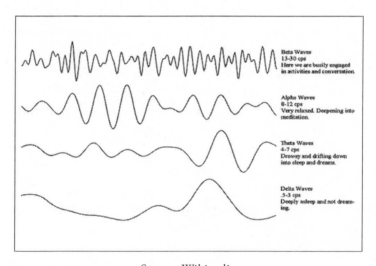

Source: Wikipedia

We are making the case for astrological influences and cycles as "choice criteria."

"The fault, dear Brutus, is not in our stars,
but in ourselves, that we are underlings."

SHAKESPEARE

The fault is not in the stars, but in the choices, we make; however, guidance to the solutions to our problems resides there.

We need a foundation for making choices in a different context than has been the norm by recognizing and accommodating the influences of natural cycles on human thinking, emotions, and choices.

We seem to have a genetic code for responding to and creating cyclical environments. When we observe a consistent pattern of activity and/or relationships, we generally consider it to be a universal principle or law. This concept is the foundation of all our science.

How to merge astrological guidance and modern analytics

The human factor. Humans try to transform the natural world and create new systems for specific results. Our inventions and interventions can result in beneficial progress, but they have expanded in frequency, speed, and influence, often without sufficient controls or objectives. ***We are now living in an age of extreme, unintended consequences that can emerge overnight.*** Many of our choices and actions misuse, ignore, or contradict the larger natural world. Human endeavors are most successful when in sync with the natural cycles. When interventions are out of sync, especially by intention, they are more likely to yield negative outcomes, as evident in the entire history of periodic wars and economic calamities. ***Are these types of extreme consequences just our nature, as some philosophize, or are they examples of when we collectively and on a large scale go against nature?***

Modern behavioral/trend analyses. We have vast amounts of data about how people behave within economic, business, social, and cultural systems. The question is this: Are the issues about which we make choices in any way influenced by external forces that are described by astrology? And, if so, how do we incorporate astrology into a new decision-making process?

Astrology is the practice and language developed to interpret astronomical patterns as they relate to observable human and environmental life. We already accept many discoveries about the laws of astronomy and physics, but we demand more proof to make the leap to astrology. We accept that sunspots disrupt electromagnetic activity and that the earth is spinning at 25,000 miles per hour and we cannot feel it. The new mysteries of dark matter/energy are profound, but we can't measure them and don't know how they work. Since we accept so many extraordinary cosmic facts of life, *is it unreasonable to believe that systematic astronomical configurations and the energy they emanate can exert influences on human biologic patterns and electrical signals, and thus our way of thinking and behavior?*

Astrological cycles are ever present and have predictable spatial combinations of the planets and stars. The sheer physical energy emanated by astronomical objects represents potential influences over other components of the electromagnetic universe - that is us.

Statisticians and scientists want large data sets to develop models and forecasts. Weather forecasting is improved because we have accumulated millions of observations or data points that are necessary to build predictive models. The same is true for astrology — thousands of years of observations connected to observable activity. But astrological values have not been quantified to be readily used in mainstream analytics. We maintain that there is enormous historical evidence for astrological validity, within its limits. And it is likely that we can establish measures that can help provide a usable scale of influences for the conditions and calendar times in which we must make choices.

We propose that it is time to reconnect natural cycles to how humans make choices and take actions. Every scientific concept was once unimaginable or even considered heretical. We want to reawaken the opportunities for using astrological influences in conjunction with modern analyses.

Humans are wired to keep score, measure, and take a temperature. We believe we can do the same with a level of quantification of astrological influences on the conditions and timing of when to make decisions that are in harmony with the greater external forces. When this book is finished we plan to begin working on a template or process to connect astrological cycles and influences using more quantitative methods.

As a researcher, I appreciate the serious astrologer's reminders that astrology does not predict exactly what will happen. Rather, astrology is a discipline which has observed consistent patterns of external conditions and their relationship with what happens on the earth — seasonal, biological, and especially important to the premise of this book, the nature of human behavior and thinking. Astrological guidance is presented as tendencies and probabilities, the same basic premise as quantum physics defines our universe. Everything exists as a probability.

There are two basic states of cyclical agreement:

1. **In sync** - when an activity is in sync and in harmony with the natural cycle. Here are cycles in sync with each other. Each type of activity may have its own characteristics such as frequency, amplitude, strength, duration, etc., but the pattern of cycles would be the same.

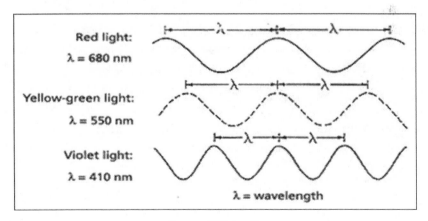

Source: Wikipedia

2. **Out of sync** - when actions that are contrary to the natural cycle will likely have opposite wave patterns and forces working against one another. But even contradictory cycles do have brief periods of overlap, denoted by the circles. So regardless of intent, human activities will very likely be in sync for a brief window of opportunity. Maybe that is what we call luck or beating the odds.

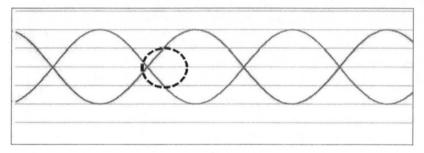

Source: 3iconexxion research llc

External cycles exist beyond our control, while the human-made cycles and interventions are generally made without regard to the natural cycles. Attempts to harness cyclical influences, whether using astrology or eclectic stock-picking methodologies, are considered novelties with little relevance to the "real world." Our goal in this book is to create a greater awareness of the tendencies of the overarching natural cycles, and make our choices and take actions to be more in harmony with the cycle. Thus...*go with the flow*.

When human cycles are in total contradiction of natural cycles, the probability of failure is far more likely than success. Periodic economic crashes must represent an extreme out-of-sync cyclical environment. We invite readers to submit their ideas and examples of cyclical analysis from their own experiences. You can contact us at our Analyst website: www.3imacroanalytics.com

Choices

The great and successful human effort has been survival - making the right choices, most of the time, in the most critical situations. But

human progress has also introduced new variables and influences that clearly interfere with our ability to make our best instinctive survival choices.

Today there is too much information to make the most efficient and beneficial choice at any point in time. And as individuals, most critical choices are based on criteria established by someone else — sometimes for the common good but very often for a proprietary interest. We have created too much urgency for making choices propelled by the continuous flow of information and, thereby, reducing the time available to make more deliberate decisions.

There is a lot of research about human behavior and taking risks, making decisions, relationships, and other aspects of making choices. We have well-developed disciplines in psychology, sociology, anthropology, and other scientifically-based disciplines. One of the most studied aspects of risk/choice behavior has been on the stock market.

We will use the financial markets as the demonstration case because stock market research has one of the largest sets of data that have been analyzed. That is because financial markets generate information literally by the minute. This information has countless variables, strategies, actions, and interventions, and we have the computer power to analyze this information and look for relationships and patterns.

But therein lies one of the problems with risk/choice behavior models — there is likely a serious flaw in what we are observing and measuring. There are well-established theories that try to define and explain economic behavior and how we make choices. Let us start with one of the most recognized, theories, prospect theory, which is widely used in current economic and financial models.

Prospect theory (*Wikipedia*)

The theory was created in 1979 and developed in 1992 by Daniel Kahneman and Amos Tversky as a psychologically more accurate description of decision making, compared to the expected utility theory. In the original formulation, the term *prospect* referred to a lottery... The paper, "Prospect Theory: An Analysis of Decision under Risk," has been called a seminal paper in behavioral economics. Kahneman won a Nobel prize in economics for his work developing Prospect theory.

Prospect theory is a behavioral economic theory that describes that people choose between probabilistic alternatives that involve risk, where the probabilities of outcomes are known. The theory states that people make decisions based on the potential value of losses and gains rather than the outcome and that people evaluate the losses and gains using certain heuristics. The model is descriptive: it tries to model real-life choices, rather than optimal decisions, as normative models do.

I generally agree with the concepts of prospect theory and have seen its propositions firsthand in my own business life. But there is a flaw that needs to be recognized and it is not just regarding prospect theory, but also many other types of similar research interest.

All research about human risk/decision theory in modern times is based on people making decisions with flawed information, unrealistic criteria, and often without adequate skills to make the optimal choice. Their experiences then factor into subsequent decisions. The situation is a fact of life.

We would not make plans for a trip based on last month's weather report, but analogously we are doing the same thing with economic behavior research.

What is occurring is that we can accurately measure truthful, but inaccurate behavior. People made a decision in good faith, based on the information available, but that information was inherently flawed in some way, which will be realized tomorrow or next month, and the consequences of the choice will not be what was expected. **This is what modern research is measuring - accurate measures of behavior made by mistake.**

Humans have evolved and survived because for thousands of years we made enough of the correct choices at the right time for survival. We do have the DNA for survival-based choices, based on the information available in the conditions with which we have been faced. We probably had to think faster with less information and trust our instincts as well as experience.

It is the natural outcome of evolving civilization that humans have become further removed from their original connections to nature. We still have hunches, gut feelings, and other built-in signals. But now the number of choices and the information available has overwhelmed the ability of our instincts to quickly and accurately act in our best interest. The control of choices is spread across too many controlling forces, with dubious information and little oversight.

Researchers use large sets of data over long periods of time to identify statistically reliable patterns. However, the original behavior they are analyzing is inherently distorted behavior.

At the simplest level, such as whether to buy a Ford or a Chevrolet, risk analysis is probably very reliable. Price, income, credit score, popularity, etc., all are considered - a finite number of variables, each with a relatively narrow range of probabilities and outcomes.

But when we scale up the analyses at the macroeconomic level, many of the decisions studied, and their outcomes have a high percentage, if not a majority, of what will likely be choices based on unreliable information.

So back to the definition of insanity, high-level economic decisions continue to be made over and over the same way, and thus the volatility of markets and periodic major and minor crashes.

It is clear to us — observing and codifying flawed behavior cannot result in reliable choice criteria, and this mechanism has not been working out too well. This brings us back to astrology.

The observable astronomical patterns described by astrology are not subject to human intervention. If there is some type of electromagnetic energy because of the alignment of planets which affects human biology and thinking, we have no control over it; humans react to those influences. **Astrological history is perhaps the purest form of historical data about external influences and related measurable human behavior.** We can now try to align our choices and the types of the decisions we make within the known or likely astrological tendencies based on these greater cosmic forces.

There is too much information to make the most efficient and beneficial choice at any point in time. Most of the critical choices in our lives are based on criteria established by someone else, sometimes for the common good but very often for a proprietary interest.

We hope we have been successful in asking you to accept that cycles are fundamental to life and that they have been validated in everything from biology to physics to astronomy. We should reinstate the patterns described by astrology as one of the quantitative and qualitative tools for how we understand the influences on our decisions.

Chapter 3

● ● ●

Economic Choices

❖ The Analyst

The biggest business on the planet is "money" in its multiple forms — from the weekly paycheck to tangible precious metals to the valuations of the stocks and bonds to ambiguous instruments such as derivatives. Economics is the discipline, art and science of studying, managing and applying money concepts. We have designated "economic choices" as the #1 factor in the extinction/evolution challenges discussed in this book - where economic value is too often more important than overall benefits for the greater good.

Economic practices, philosophies, and systems operate at many levels and touch every person. We will focus primarily on the economic behavior in the United States for which we have most data. Economic challenges extend throughout the world, but humanity cannot choose the most beneficial paths if the United States is not the primary catalyst for economic change.

Trends, challenges, forecasts, and opportunities

*   For the foreseeable future, economic conditions and cycles will become more volatile and frequent, disrupting financial markets and business planning. The ripple effect will extend to employment, interest rates, business investment, and even more political conflicts.

* Income disparity will accelerate social conflict and diminish consumption capacity - the self-inflicted damage of disparity. Disparity will continue to grow and lead to political and social confrontations, especially for the 2018/2020 elections.

* The economic version of MAD (Mutually Assured Destruction with nuclear war) is already apparent - economic leverage is no longer a U.S. exclusive.

* The U.S. dollar will encounter more pressure as the major reserve currency, as current political confusion enables unplanned gifts to other blocs. The dollar is still the primary global currency, but is now one of five major reserves (United States Dollar, European Euro, British Pound, Japanese Yen, Chinese Yuan), and is in danger of being outnumbered by currency competition.

* There will be a reordering of priorities after the next big crash, somewhere from late 2017 to 2019 before the next presidential election, and which will be the sole political recalibration.

* The Trump effect:
    * If Trump policies are largely effective, the world economic order will be reset/recalibrated and global economic and trade relations will change with unknown consequences.
    * If Trump policies largely fail, the world economic order will be highly volatile and chaotic for several years, U.S. policies will be weakened, and China, Europe, and Russia will try to make further inroads.

* Our concerns and forecasts are not intended to be presented as a new formula for socialism or any failed economic ideology. Our goal is to have intelligent, widespread democratic capitalism where both the few and the many can prosper and be rewarded.

*"Infinite growth of material consumption
in a finite world is an impossibility."*

E.F. Schumacher

Economic criteria are the foundation of most critical choices today and they most often are set and controlled by narrow and self-perpetuating economic interests. If we are to escape the "extinction" trajectory, we need to make more economic choices for the greater good. There is no inherent problem with capitalism - making a profit or return on investment. This economics theory is fundamental to ensuring that there are resources to support the necessary structures of life. But current conditions around the world demonstrate the lagging or even regressing economic progress of the individuals.

Economic Choices

At any point in time there are a finite amount of economic resources in the world and their allocation directly affects the very real decisions that are life-and-death, from medical care to clean energy technologies.

The priority needs for "greater good" economic choices include:

*   Economic disparity. What level is acceptable as a reward for economic success and how much equality is necessary for a sustainable and robust economy?
*   The 70% consumer-demand U.S. Economy. Increased income disparity, low wages, and increases in productivity will result in fewer jobs and lower average wages. As the total consumption capacity decreases, the growth of absolute buying will decrease, only matched to population change at best.
*   Reliability of financial instruments. Options, margins, derivatives, risk models, etc., cumulatively and collectively are again

increasing in use with little or no control. Volatility is the poison of reliability.

* Domination of uncertainty in economic psychology and behavior. Uncertainty has become the new normal, but it is extremely fragile. Information speed and contradiction feed volatility and accelerate and increase potential negative impacts. How do we measure and manage uncertainty?

* Short-term business financial objectives and quarterly goals. In a weakened economy we will need more pragmatic assessment methods to evaluate and reward corporate performance that is less susceptible to manipulation and expediency.

* Increased automation and related technologies. While these are a legitimate pursuit of profits, they will further reduce employment of human workers and lower the average wage. Technology-based productivity is progressing faster than job creation, job retraining, general education, and more.

* Highly variable/manipulated energy economics. These outcomes lead to increased costs directly affecting consumer demand and quality of life. Conventional energy does have a large infrastructure and capital base which cannot easily be transformed quickly. There must be the wisdom and will to make energy conversion a global priority. Many countries have recognized the future of energy needs and are working on alternatives more quickly than the United States. Energy opportunities could and should be one of the top survival economic choices.

Economic goals and investment need these updated choice criteria:

* Improving rather than diminishing the standard of living with emphasis on wages, healthcare, education, and affordable housing.
* Directing job creation.
* Providing sufficient investment to maintain the capital formation process and fair profits.

There are several sectors that have immediate needs which can provide immediate benefits and job creation and address several global challenges. These are the sectors that will drive future investment opportunities:

* New energy sources for manufacturing, agriculture, transportation, environmental management, heating/cooling.
* Healthcare without a profit-only motive.
* Environmental realignment that is not about "tree hugging" but about technologies to manage resources helpful to humans and which provides stability in the ecosystem.
* Agricultural efficiency adapted to climate change and water for survival.
* Education that must both expand and be redirected to support the critical economic transformations.

Excessive investment in "thin sectors" is a zero-sum game. Social media is the best example. There is a finite capacity in how much people can use technologies for social media, to talk, text, share pictures, and shop online. There is also a corresponding finite level of advertising support. Over the next five to ten years there will be a plateauing and reconfiguration of social media economics.

In contrast, investments in renewable opportunities such as energy, agriculture, and healthcare are not a zero-sum game. There is perpetual growth in the population base and an immense global backlog of fulfilling needs for education, healthcare, food, and safety.

Financial markets are now based primarily on uncertainty and are very fragile. Traditional investment concepts have been transformed by the quantitative models to take risks based on probabilities and speed rather than the inherent value of the investment. The actual accuracy of choice is less important than the outcome, hence the "greater fool theory." Once again, we emphasize that volatility is the "canary in the coal mine" of fragility.

It is highly likely that between late 2017 to 2019 there will be another financial collapse that might finally mobilize regulation, responsibility, transparency, and consumer protection. Financial stresses will be the highlight of the presidential election in 2020, and we will see the economic confrontation begin well before the 2018 elections. The third meltdown of significant size within 20 years will not be tolerated (2000, 2008, and 2020). Capitalism and investments are necessary and can be beneficial. More data, moving faster with more convoluted risk models, will only aggravate the situation and increase the probability of more financial blackouts. **Financial markets are one of the prime targets of cyber warfare.**

There are two major areas of economic threats that might supersede, at least in the short term, all others:

1. **Economic Mutually Assured Destruction (E-MAD).**
2. **Financial market roulette.**

E-MAD represents the intricately linked financial connections that enable the global economy. The connections include trade, control of scarce resources, currency exchange, and extraordinary credit and debt. Politicians continue with empty threats of economic sanctions which might work for the very smallest and economically defenseless countries, certainly not for China. The reality is that the U.S. debt, approaching $20 trillion, can never be paid off with almost half held by foreign entities, and with China arguably the largest holder of U.S. investments of all types. The economic/leverage warfare is a minimal tool for the U.S. today because every other country in the world is better able to deal with economic deprivation than the United States. China, Russia, and the Middle East already have lower standards of living and have had more experience in dealing with widespread economic calamities.

The fragility of the U.S. and global economy has numerous examples. Several years ago, the Greek debt crisis threatened to bring down the European economy and affect the U.S. There are many other countries which still have significant economic connections that can ripple out to other economies.

New words have entered our lexicon and appear with unfortunate regularity — fiscal cliff, debt ceiling, government shutdown, and sovereign debt. From political parties, we continually hear promises of economic prosperity, but the headlines warn of U.S. defaults and government shutdowns. This is not a sustainable economic environment.

Stock markets are no longer a matter of traditional investment, but are high-speed, high-risk asset transformation and, unfortunately, entertainment. There is a familiar anecdote about Joseph Kennedy before the 1929 stock market crash. As the story goes, Kennedy was getting his shoes shined and the boy was talking about investment advice. Kennedy recognized this as a signal that the bubble was about to burst. Similarly, much of the daily news and entire networks are devoted to business and the stock market. This is just a more sophisticated version of the shoeshine syndrome — when everybody knows, nobody will win. Financial markets are still critical to economic development and are not going away. Therefore, it is worth a brief review of the nature of the markets.

We focus on the U.S. stock market as the most dramatic and insightful example of economic threats. Whatever happens in the stock market immediately spills over into every other sector of consumer and business environment. It clearly happened in 2008. There have been smaller crashes and recessions over the decade. Current activity and trends indicate to us an addiction to financial market roulette.

For the past 15 years Richard has run a macro-economic trend analysis business. As we noted, "the clues were in the news," and then we need another cliché to describe what happened - the proverbial "tipping" point.

Macro-trend data showed a clear shift in sentiment beginning in 2006, fully two years before the economy fell off the cliff. The economy has recovered far more quickly than expected due to a combination of government intervention, low interest rates, and continued easy credit. But the economy has recovered without full conviction — the dominant measurement in our data was and remains "uncertainty."

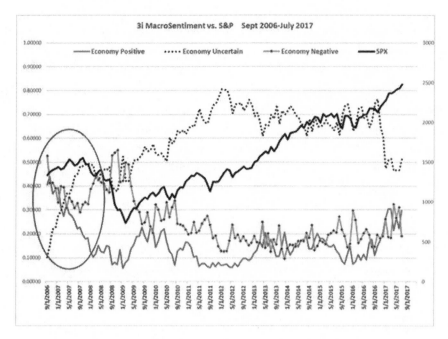

Source: 3iconexxion research llc. www.3imacroanalytics.com

Employing asset strategies that recognize the influences of external cycles and meet these criteria for the "greater good" will be a distinct competitive advantage for years to come. This philosophy would be great if it were the norm, but we are realistic — relatively few people will take advantage of our proposed astrological/analytic recommendations. Some people who will employ our recommendations will do so for money, not necessarily altruistic reasons. But if the results are beneficial to all, this is an excellent first step.

Our short dissertation focuses on two theories that are considered the major economic philosophies of the financial markets:

1. Efficient market hypothesis (EMH).
2. Behavioral finance (BF).

We can observe and measure but can rarely predict the volatility and direction of markets. The markets are not quite as mysterious as "dark matter," but they are still at the mercy of both the natural and human-made cycles.

As investing and economic analysis became mainstream in the 1950s, the efficient market hypothesis emerged. EMH says the financial markets generally make the most efficient decision because all information is available, part of decision criteria, and everybody would follow this reasonable approach. There are points in time where it seemed individuals and markets follow EMH principles, and the premise was accepted that most people act in their best interest most of the time and the markets generally operated in a coherent manner. But every crash and increasing volatility challenge the validity and durability of the theory.

Efficient-market hypothesis (*Wikipedia*)
Efficient-market hypothesis (EMH) is a theory in financial economics that states that an asset's prices fully reflect all available information. A direct implication is that it is impossible to "beat the market" consistently on a risk-adjusted basis since market prices should only react to new information or changes in discount rates (the latter may be predictable or unpredictable).

The EMH was developed by Professor Eugene Fama who argued that stocks always trade at their fair value, making it impossible for investors to either purchase undervalued stocks or sell stocks for inflated prices. As such, it should be impossible to outperform the overall market through expert stock selection or market timing, and that the only way an investor can possibly obtain higher returns is by chance or by purchasing riskier investments.[1] His 2012 study with Kenneth French confirmed this view, showing that the distribution of abnormal returns of US mutual funds is very similar to what would be expected if no fund managers had any skill—a necessary condition for the EMH to hold.

Despite the serious and quantitative nature of EMH, there was an anecdotal version of the way markets work, and perhaps the most entertaining, the "greater fool theory." Basically, I can take risks today because I'll always be able to sell it to somebody else tomorrow

Greater fool theory (*Wikipedia*)
The greater fool theory states that the price of an object is determined not by its intrinsic value, but rather by irrational beliefs and expectations of market participants. A price can be justified by a rational buyer under the belief that another party is willing to pay an even higher price. In other words, one may pay a price that seems "foolishly" high because one may rationally have the expectation that the item can be resold to a "greater fool" later.

The scientific validation of the greater fool theory was developed more recently and is called behavioral finance. I believe this is the pervasive and prevailing mechanism in operation today despite the many people who still support the EMH.

Behavioral finance. As the financial markets became as much entertainment as capitalism, and information exploded, another theory was put forth and popularized by Robert Schiller of Yale, the concept of behavioral finance. Some of the principles go back to the ideas of John Maynard Keynes. My favorite Keynesian observation is that the stock market is like a beauty contest. The best way to predict the winner of the contest is not to personally make a choice, but to try and determine who the judges will pick based on their criteria. What you think is irrelevant. You must be accurate about what the decision-makers think. Behavioral finance is described as economic and financial decisions being made by both tangible and intangible, quantitative and qualitative criteria — numbers, psychology of the participants, emotional stresses, and riskier strategies.

Behavioral Economics (Wikipedia)
Behavioral economics, along with behavioral finance, studies the effects of psychological, social, cognitive, and emotional factors on the economic decisions of individuals and institutions and the consequences for market prices, returns, and resource allocation, although not always that narrowly, but also more generally, of the impact of different kinds of behavior, in different environments of varying experimental values.

Risk tolerance is a crucial factor in personal financial decision making. Risk tolerance is defined as individuals' willingness to engage in a financial activity whose outcome is uncertain.

Behavioral economics is primarily concerned with the bounds of rationality of economic agents. Behavioral models typically integrate insights from psychology, neuroscience, and microeconomic theory; in so doing, these behavioral models cover a range of concepts, methods, and fields.

The study of behavioral economics includes how market decisions are made and the mechanisms that drive public choice. The use of the term "behavioral economics" in U.S. scholarly papers has increased in the past few years, as shown by a recent study.

Guess what history has shown? Both theories are right!
The fascinating outcome of the competing theories is that their originators, Eugene Fama (EMH) and Robert Schiller and Lars Hansen (BF), were jointly awarded the Nobel Prize for economics in 2013 because both theories were correct at different points in time and often overlap depending upon criteria.

My analysis: EMH used to be the most relevant theory when there was less and slower moving information, but that age has passed. We

are fully in the age of 24/7 information influence on economic behavior and we have no models or methods to manage what has been created.

An excellent book about the nature of financial markets is *Fooled by Randomness* (Nissim Taleb, 2001). Taleb identifies performance in the financial markets and the accuracy of individuals as governed by the same statistical probabilities for most everything throughout the universe, portrayed in the familiar normal distribution or bell-shaped curve. It is guaranteed that there will be exceptional winners and exceptional losers and most everyone will be in the middle.

If the markets represent paper wealth and speculation, actual personal income is the core of the economy.

Income disparity and related social consequences can bring down an entire economic system. This has happened consistently throughout history.

Despite our progress in technology and in many quality-of-life areas, we still have an upside-down view of economic priorities. Profit for a few is more important than prosperity for all, and this is true throughout the world. There may be a few pockets of relative economic equality, such as in Scandinavia, but these conditions are dismissed as socialism. But the irony is that widespread prosperity is what fuels the profit. Economic power for the many is what creates the greater economic rewards for the few. The more people who can buy new houses, new cars, new TVs and take more trips generate more wealth for those who own and provide those material goods.

Wealth hoarding is a self-destructive concept — pressures on the buying power of the consumer eventually results in reduced consumption. The wildcard in this formula, unfortunately, is in the form of credit. Consumers do not have enough income to pay for all that we buy. The neglected reality is that we want our source of prosperity to be sustained and to grow, not to be increasingly pressured and reduced.

We are now at a point where income disparity and uneven distribution of resources is universally known and can no longer be hidden. The movements of a few years ago after the 2008 recession, such as Occupy Wall Street, had the right ideas but inadequate organization and faced active resistance among the establishment. But in some form the right to economic survival will reassert itself as current political and business structures fail to recognize this threat to their own existence.

• • •

❖ The Astrologer

A Look at Recent History

Unless you have been living alone on a distant mountaintop somewhere, it is common knowledge that the current globalized economic policies and structures are not working for most people throughout the world and certainly for about half of the population here in the U.S., who currently live at or below the poverty line. Those of us who comprise roughly 48% of the population enjoy a degree of prosperity, but are frequently afraid that global financial instabilities could erase our economic security from one day to the next. The notable exception to this is the infamous 1% that own or control approximately 80 - 90 % of the global wealth, depending upon which source and which time the projection is published.

An article was published on *AlterNet* entitled, "Now Five Men Own Almost as Much Wealth as Half of the World's Population," (Paul Bucheit, June 12, 2017). Bucheit writes: "An analysis of 2016 data found that the poorest five deciles of the world population own about $410 billion in total wealth. As of June 8, 2017, the world's richest five men owned over $400 billion in wealth. Thus, on average, each man owns nearly as much as 750 million people." Bucheit goes on to say: "In 2016 alone, the richest 1% effectively shifted nearly $4 trillion in wealth away from the nation to themselves, with nearly ½ of the wealth transfer ($1.94 trillion) coming from the nation's poorest 90% - the middle and lower classes."

The Great Wave – Pluto conjunct Saturn

Arguably, since the last **Pluto/Saturn conjunction in the sign of Libra** in 1982, here in the U.S., we have witnessed a trend of government deregulation of the private sector, reduction of taxation for giant corporations and banking institutions, and a movement of assets of people wealthy enough to "off-shore" their wealth to tax havens. In 2016, information was released concerning billionaires offshoring their money to overseas tax havens that is now referred to as the "Panama Papers" scandal with 11 million pages containing the names of hundreds of Americans.

As corporations moved manufacturing out of the U.S., they have been able to reduce their taxes by offshoring these obligations and hiring cheap labor from parts of the world whose majority population lives in destitution and who have no environmental restrictions. The spin from Washington "conservatives" the past several years has been that the U.S. is "broke" and can no longer afford Medicaid, Medicare, and Social Security, and services to the public in general is propaganda of the first order. If these hugely wealthy people paid their taxes like the rest of us, we could have increased fiscal stability and could afford to support the national public at large.

The planet **Pluto** is symbolic of the segment of the population which has concentrated wealth and power, whether this is a central government, giant banks, or large corporations. **Saturn** is associated with order and the structure of societies' institutions, i.e., what is known as "the establishment." **Pluto's transit in the sign of Capricorn** from 2008 to 2023/24 suggests a highly centralized control brought about by the collusion of governments with giant banks and global corporations, moving away from the notion of more democratic economies and a tax-subsidized public infrastructure. It suggests movements of money into securities (stocks and bonds), hedge funds (derivatives), and real estate rather than into wages and salaries, the pockets of the public-at-large, and/or private savings. Thus, we have what some refer to as a "financialized" economy.

The middle class on life supports

The outsourcing of manufacturing labor to relatively destitute people in developing nations and automation of tasks to robots and computers have eliminated whole professions and sectors of the economy, leading to a major decline in what we are accustomed to calling "the middle class." Interestingly, French economist, Thomas Piketty, in his bestselling book, *Capital in the Twenty-first Century*, (2014) presents evidence that the theory of "equal opportunity" is an ideological illusion under the supposedly free-market capitalism economy. He uses statistical analysis to demonstrate that capital and its owners have always tended to produce ever larger inequalities and that material inequalities have been sustained and grown by the reproduction of financial wealth for two centuries. In addition, definitions as to who and what constitute the middle class are wide and varied, and there is little or no evidence that people who perceive themselves as middle class are willing to participate in reforms in societies to create a more equal playing field and reduce poverty.

In recent years, a widespread corporate practice of "marketization" and "financialization" has mushroomed. This includes the practice of companies firing employees with Ph.D.'s who had helped build innovation in favor of less educated, inexpensive foreign labor and the practice of instituting stock "buybacks" and stock options for upper level employees bringing stock prices up and masking less innovation and profit. All this has contributed to a kind of Ponzi scheme destined for failure. Historically, low interest rates have discouraged saving and moved more money into the stock market. These decisions and practices increase corporate "bottom line" savings (cheap labor) and bring on temporary highs in equities while devastating the job market and public infrastructure.

Colleges and universities are now run like profits-only corporations, raising tuitions to all-time highs which led to an unprecedented burden of debt for students. Recently it has been reported that indebtedness is ballooning due to increases in credit card loans, auto loans, and college loans that is affecting an entire generation of young people.

Wages have fallen or stagnated. A shocking study, *The Rise and Nature of Alternative Work Arrangements in the United States*, 1995-2015 (Lawrence Katz of Harvard University & Alan Krueger of Princeton University, March, 2016) states that 94% of the jobs added to the U.S. economy in the past decade are temporary, part-time, or contracting jobs. Many are extremely low paying, located in "service" industries and might be referred to as "jobettes." Some refer to this as the "gig economy." Yet the official unemployment figure at the time of this writing is just over 4%. This does not count people who have given up looking for employment in areas that lost manufacturing jobs, or those whose unemployment has run out, or people who have been chronically unemployed for many years.

Thousands of homeless people have been migrating across the U.S. to the more temperate climate zones in Washington, Oregon, and California, living in the parks, bushes, and wooded areas. Some are actually employed but cannot afford the rents in these areas that have been rising to unprecedented highs in the past decade.

Health care costs have been rising. The U.S. pays more for health care than any other developed nation and provides less coverage. An aging and surviving population in the U.S., combined with fewer people employed and thus paying taxes, have conspired to create a system that is no longer working, even after the attempts of President Obama's "Affordable Health Care Act" to provide insurance for most people and the Trump administration's failed attempts to dismantle and replace it.

Populist uprising - The revolutionary square of Pluto (wealth and power) to Uranus (mavericks) (2011 – 2015)

The rising tide of discontent resulted in a U.S. presidential election in 2016 of a "so-called" populist maverick, who is a master media manipulator assisted by a media that exists for ratings only, and the loudest, most sensational mouthpiece. His opponent was seen as an insider who appeared to be complicit with the "takeover" of the rich and powerful and did not represent the population-at-large. So, a rich and powerful man who "games" the system was elected amidst the most hate-mongering, finger-pointing, immigrant-blaming, scandal-infested campaign in recent history. In addition to all this, an ongoing investigation by the FBI and CIA points to hacking by Russia to influence the election to favor President Trump that has, at the time of this writing, expanded into a vast scandal implicating the President and his family and associates.

It is understandable why so many people decided to vote for someone they perceived existed outside of institutions they no longer trusted. The "Brexit" vote in the United Kingdom (UK) and close elections in The Netherlands and France with challenging "populist" candidates, have reflected the disillusionment of populations in nations throughout the world. The revolutions toppling governments in the petrochemical-dependent economies in the regions of the Middle East have resulted in autocrats taking over in Egypt and Turkey. Syria is still fighting a devastating civil war with the military dictator, Assad. Venezuela, another petroleum-dependent economy, has been taken over by a dictator. History tells us that when people perceive the economy is failing to work for them and their institutions are failing to operate on their behalf, these upheavals are often the result.

In addition to all this, we are witnessing significant threats to the solvency of many economies due to unsustainable sovereign debt (U.S. debt is currently around $20 trillion), the effects of global climate extremities (the worst drought in Syria in recorded history, Hurricane Harvey and its all-time record flood in Texas, and Hurricanes Irma and Maria, the most powerful ever recorded), and the seemingly endless costly military invasions and occupations by the U.S. These events have resulted in many nations in the region of the Middle East exploding into a series of ethnic civil wars and a rising of terror groups such as ISIS (Islamic State of Iraq and Syria). A positive trend in recent years is that oil prices have fallen in this region as the result of increased oil and gas production in America and new non-fossil fuel energy technologies being developed and implemented around the world. This has resulted in a cycle of "energy deflation."

As an astrologer, I see these waves of discontent in the U.S. and around the world coinciding with the recent **Pluto/Uranus square** (that previously occurred in the 1930s) and the after effects that are continuing until the mid-2020s. In my previous books, I have referred to this cycle as a "Great

Depression" for many people and an atmosphere that may bring about "the second American Revolution." Obviously, these ethnic, civil, and populist revolutions have been expressed in a variety of ways throughout many nations. Multiple public protests have been launched in the past several years throughout the U.S. involving the "Occupy Wall Street" demonstrations, the "Black Lives Matter" movement, the "Women's Equality" movement in Washington, D.C. following the presidential inauguration, the Native American tribes protecting their land and water rights from oil pipeline projects, to the "White Supremacist" and "Neo-Nazi" organizations protesting the removal of a statue of Robert E. Lee in Virginia.

Is Our System Working?

Financial markets, supply and demand for products and services, ownership, assumption of debt, and speculation are at the heart of the modern Capitalist system which has been known to work well when balanced with government-instituted rule of law, reducing criminal activities and monopolies that become so manipulative and powerful that they literally walk over the corpses of everyone outside their conclave. The notion of "checks and balances" between private enterprise and elected government are known to keep powers in check. Since 1913, the creation of the Federal Reserve moved discretionary monetary policy from Washington to the private bankers and Wall Street, with some government oversite supposedly supplied by a presidential appointment of a Chair of the Federal Reserve. After the 1929 Crash on Wall Street during the Roosevelt years, the Glass-Steagall Act was passed separating investment banks from traditional lending banks to protect the nation against the banking failures that preceded it. This protection was abolished in the 1990s. Global trading agreements such as NAFTA (North American Free Trade Agreement) were passed. We all know what happened in 2007 - 2008 after the sub-prime real estate lending debacle, the crash in global derivatives, and their combined threats to the banking system. We know that the ensuing bailouts were assumed by American taxpayers. Following the "crash" on Wall Street, the banking system was "saved" and, despite the feeble Dodd-Frank legislation, no meaningful regulation was re-instituted. At the time of the writing of this book there is talk of more deregulation on Wall Street.

Follow the money

In recent years, banks have obtained much of their wealth through capital gains (real estate, stocks, and bonds) plus high investment fees rather than from interest from lending. This has led to policies to inflate assets more than providing credit for small businesses or interest for savers. High risk hedge funds have been developed that currently trade in hundreds of trillions of dollars of derivative contracts formed within the context of a high-risk global "casino." As an astrologer looking at trends and cycles, I have observed that since the **Saturn/Pluto conjunction in Libra** in November 1982, there has been a noticeable and coherent movement toward the government getting "bought out" by the very rich corporations, especially the giant banks who are linked to the Federal Reserve system in the U.S. since its inception in 1913. Both political parties are complicit. Political campaigns are financed by the money-laden and this was reinforced by the **Pluto/Saturn square in Capricorn** (the establishment) and **Libra** (the law and the courts) in 2010 when the famous "Citizens United" case was ruled upon by the U.S. Supreme Court. This case simply gave the corporations and banks the right to spend a virtually unlimited amount of money on political campaigns, referring to this as "freedom of speech." **Pluto** symbolizes concentrated wealth and power and **Saturn** is about established structures and institutions.

Politics and the economy are wrapped around each other, are embattled, enmeshed, are "frenemies," enablers, helpers, and mutual assassins. **Pluto** is a planet that symbolizes the use and abuse of power, the death of the previous system, and the birth of a new one. **Saturn** is symbolic of structure, organization, and authority. When they aspect one another, particularly in a conjunction, we watch the old ideals, power structures, and institutions die and new ones arise. Giant "spin" campaigns are effectively launched stating that the old system is irrelevant, non-profitable, outworn, and that the new one represents "freedom, liberty, and prosperity for all." In reality, the richest and most powerful attain more riches and more power. The "get the government out of our lives and let corporate profits roll in" Reagan Revolution spoke to this. It was framed and highlighted by the famous climax in the movie, *Wall Street*, (1987) when the anti-hero Gordon Gekko states: "Greed is good"!

The new "Gilded Age"

In recent years, we have witnessed a takeover by monopolies not seen since the turn of the 20th Century, the famous Gilded Age of the "Robber Barons." Both inequality in wealth and an environment that creates an unequal playing field have been dramatically increasing over the past 30 years. On Wall Street, billions of dollars, even trillions in assets, are in the hands of a relative handful of mutual funds, concentrating investments of retirement funds and savings to an extent that has never been seen before. In the on-line newsletter, *The Conversation*, an article was published entitled, "These Three Firms Own Corporate America" (Fichtner, Heemskerk, & Garcia-Bernardo, May 10, 2107). These authors state that: "Fundamental change is underway in stock market investing and the spin-off effects are poised to dramatically impact corporate America." They reveal that the three giant American asset managers are Blackrock, Vanguard, and State Street. They add that: "The magnitude of the change is astounding: from 2007 to 2016, actively managed funds have recorded outflows of roughly US $1,200 billion, while index funds had inflows of over US $1,400 billion. In the first quarter of 2017, index funds brought in more than US $200 billion, the highest quarterly value on record." In addition to all this, giant banks, in league with the Federal Reserve, are trading literally trillions of dollars in derivatives that are complex contracts that buy and sell "bets" on commodities, stocks, and even markets. When they lie about their losses, they get "slap-on-the-wrist" fines and escape oversight and regulations that used to be in place.

Since the late 1970s, the average worker's wage has either stagnated or moved down when accounting for inflation, while profits at the top of the food chain have multiplied. Small innovative enterprises are frequently bought out and taken over by the giants. In the U.S., just one example of this is the absorption of multiple airlines into only four companies, giving them power to continually raise prices, charge large fees for checking luggage, and even drag a person bodily off a United Airlines overbooked flight. Healthy competition and accountability seem to be "things of the past."

Between 2016 and 2017 Microsoft acquired Linked In; Sherwin Williams took over Valspar; North Star Asset Management Group merged with North Star Realty and Colony Capital; ITC Holdings acquired Fortia; ADT acquired Protection 1; IMS Health Holdings merged with Quintiles Transnational Holdings; Trans Canada bought Columbia Pipeline Group (Keystone XL Pipeline); Marriott International bought Starwood to become the world's largest hotel chain; Johnson Controls bought Tyco (an Irish company to escape U.S. taxes); Abbott Laboratories bid to buy St. Jude Medical; AT&T bid to buy Time Warner; Bayer and Monsanto sought a merger; British American Tobacco sought a merger with Reynolds American; Syngenta (Swiss company) seeks to merge with Chem China; Angie's List seeks to merge with Home Advisor; and Sinclair is in talks to buy the Tribune Media Company. Giant Amazon has bought Whole Foods, an enormously important acquisition that has gotten people's collective attention and its CEO, Jeff Bezos, recently acquired *The Washington Post*.

All of this is leading us into a centralized control by transnational corporations, media monopolies, and enormous financial institutions. The trend is leading us away from the regulation and protection of sovereign laws of nations, large companies paying their taxes to their nations of origin, healthy competition, and general accountability to the populace. The failure to provide decent health care to the populace is framed by medical insurance companies and pharmaceutical industries hiking prices that have consistently put "profits before lives." It is widely known that some form of a single payer health insurance system would cost individuals and corporations much less money since they would not have to insure their employees and could afford to hire American workers.

"So-called" trade agreements such as the North American Free Trade Agreement (NAFTA) contain clauses that allow a corporation to sue a country in an "international tribunal" for whatever they (the company) interpret as "inhibiting their profits." A recent example of this was the giant oil corporation, Trans-Canada, suing the U.S. through the NAFTA agreement, for stopping the extension of the tar sands XL Pipeline when President Obama was president. President Trump has since given permission to go ahead with this pipeline. **PLUTO** (power) **in Capricorn** has solidified a trend that has been going on for many years and as **SATURN** (structure) enters this sign in December 2017, the consequences of all this will become evident.

Economies of the Future: Shock and Awe

Most of us now know that the future of employment itself is threatened by one primary historic wave - automation. Robots and computers are already replacing people and this trend will rapidly accelerate into the future. Let us look at what is already happening. Driverless cars and trucks and delivery drones have been manufactured and tested in recent years and are now ready to go. About 50% of the men employed in the U.S. drive a vehicle for a living and are set to lose their jobs. In the field of medicine, robot surgeries are already being used and more are being developed. Amazon, in addition to its influence in dramatically reducing bricks and mortar stores leading to the projected closings of about 300 mall stores throughout the U.S., has recently gone into the grocery business and will deliver food directly to people, eliminating millions of jobs in supermarkets throughout the nation. Other companies, including Martha Stewart, Inc., and Walmart are following this trend. Many corporations are complaining they cannot fill the jobs needed, but they continue to pay such low wages that those who are technically "employed" cannot afford to support themselves. The gap between pay for CEOs and the average worker has and is still expanding to all-time highs.

At this moment in time, many people see no future for themselves unless they are a small percentage of highly educated engineers who are creating these advanced machines and even these people may be eventually putting themselves out of business by replacing themselves with their own "creations." We will cover more of this in our chapter about technology later in this book, but it is important to note that these topics are entwined and immersed in a matrix of evolving global economies that will not function at all unless we address the coming "tech tsunami."

What next?

This book is being written in 2017. By the end of this year, I would predict at the very least a significant "correction" and possibly a "crash" in financial markets generating a recession as **Saturn moves** from the Galactic Center **into the sign of Capricorn**. However, the larger wave changer will be the **Pluto/Saturn conjunction at 22 degrees Capricorn** January 12, 2020, reawakening the 1993 **Uranus/Neptune** (technology expansion) **conjunction at 19 degrees Capricorn** (the signing of NAFTA (North American Free Trade Agreement), the Internet revolution, and the advent of "globalism"), and will *supplant* the Great Wave of the **Pluto/Saturn conjunction** of 1982. **Jupiter conjuncts Pluto** in April of 2020, all presaging the USA's **Pluto** "return" in its birth chart (July 4, 1776). The last time this astrological event occurred, we formed a new nation and fought a revolution against Great Britain and its monarchy. This time, the "people" may rebel against the current corporate ruling "elite" who are enthroned in power in America itself. Remember the call, "taxation without representation"? Ironically, "Mad King George" was the ruling monarch in Great Britain during that period. History may not repeat itself, but it rhymes!

Capricorn is a sign that directs power and accountability to the current "establishment." Some people refer to this alliance between banks, giant corporations and the government (especially the military) as "the

Deep State." What differentiates this time period is that the public, who knew the identity of King George in the 1770s, frequently does not know who most of these men and women in power really are today. They keep themselves out of the spotlight. Instead, the population-at-large has been susceptible to corporate-financed political parties winning elections using racism, hate-mongering, and the age-old tendency to throw the blame for their social and economic displacements upon those of different races, sexual orientations, religions, and nationalities. The rise of the Third Reich in Germany in the 1930s reminds us that Germany's economic woes were blamed on the Jewish population which led to the great Holocaust of the 20th century.

A major trend changer will be the **Jupiter /Saturn conjunction in Aquarius** in December of 2020, reversing the political tides that have dominated our discourse since 1982. **Aquarius** is a sign that is concerned with equal opportunity, advanced technology, and the notion of democracy. However, the "down side" of the advent of the Internet and the public's burgeoning access to information through their mobile devices has presented an opportunity for corporations and various institutions to mine data about the hundreds of millions of participants. This gives companies and political campaigns the ability to "brainwash" people by targeting their emotions and private situations in life that are no longer confidential, to push their products, and to influence their votes. The ability for persons both domestic and foreign, to hack into emails and data of citizens, companies, and even government space on the internet is mind-boggling. Privacy and/or information security may be a "thing of the past."

The many failures to broadly fund education, a corporate profits-driven media that has frequently abandoned responsible fact-checked information, a removal of civics courses from most of the school systems, and a general lack of critical thinking on the part of the public are all combining to pose the greatest threats to a democratic system of government that depends for its very existence upon an informed citizenry.

The sign of **Capricorn** is symbolic of where wealth and power (government and industry) are consolidated. The coming **conjunctions of Saturn** (structure), **and Pluto** (concentrated power) **in Capricorn** in January of 2020 and **Jupiter** (expansion) **conjunct Pluto** in April of 2020 will make it apparent that the self- absorption and greed of those in the largest positions of wealth and power are behind a landscape of economic despair, environmental destruction, and massive deception. Already in 2017, as **Saturn** reaches the center of the galaxy where it last transited in 1987, auto industry profits are starting to fall and the Dow is reaching a record "peak" – all classic symptoms of a coming recession or depression. **Capricorn** is a sign of realism and most people will realize that the system, along with its leaders, will have to significantly change its course. However, the established thrones of power will fight forcefully to hold onto their power and economic supremacy. I think this critical "down cycle" will last until the mid-2020s when a true recovery may manifest.

Past Consequences and Future Choices

A serious downside to this conjunction is the tendency to get into global wars in order for the elites to retain power over resources, mainly oil deposits, pipelines, and water ways and then subsidize corporations who make weapons of war, and "whip up" a patriotism that suspends people's judgment. The **conjunction** of **Pluto** and **Saturn** in **Libra** (the law) in 1982 led us into ensuing multiple military conflicts in Eastern Europe and the Middle East. Previous to this, the U.S. had experienced the impact of the Iranian Revolution of the 1970s, skyrocketing oil prices, disconnection from the gold standard, high interest rates in order to control inflation, and recessions that continued until 1984. There was a movement to develop solar panels in this period, but most of the patents on this technology were bought by oil companies and deliberately kept out of the market place. The consequences of our interferences and involvements in the oil- rich Gulf nations escalated to the first Iraq war in 1991, resulted in the attack on America by terrorists on 9/11 in 2001 mostly by Saudi Sunni extremists, the war in Afghanistan (the longest war in our history), and the U.S. invasion of Iraq in 2003. Many nations in Central and South America have also been devastated both financially and environmentally by the lingering effects of colonialism, criminal drug cartels, and the trans-global mining and mineral interests.

The need for oil, gas, and rare earths forms a monumental portion of the machine that drives global economies. As we speak, the U.S. is supplying arms to our "so-called" ally, Saudi Arabia, for their genocidal massacre in Yemen so that they can take control of this nation whose current leadership is a client of Shia Iran. The civil war in Syria is a bloodbath that has put us in conflict with Russia who supports the Assad regime because it has historically guaranteed them their pipelines and waterways. Immediately preceding this civil war was the worst drought in recorded history in Syria. At this time, over 65 million people around the world are refugees who are fleeing famine, climate change, and war - the worst refugee crisis since World War II. Recently, Saudi Arabia, a Sunni nation, declared Qatar, a nation in which U.S. troops are stationed, to be a Shia terrorist-sponsoring state. The nuclear inspection agreement the U.S. and many other nations reached with Iran is now threatened. The complexities of dealing in this region are so enormous as to defy reason.

China is the rising "giant" in global economies, military might, and influence. It now has an equal seat at the table with the U.S. and is undeniably challenging its supremacy by trading in its own currency, purchasing land and resources all over the world, and refusing to bow down to America in the dispute over the China Sea (where they are currently drilling for oil), the current crisis in North Korea, or new trade rules proposed regarding patents and toll positions for American products. Past history has taught us that when a new power rises and challenges the reigning power, terrible wars are often the result. I do not believe China wants to engage in a world war with the U.S., but it is insisting on being in control in its regional territory. Disputes over the sovereignty of Taiwan or North Korea's launching nuclear warheads could be "trigger mechanisms" for a military conflict that no rational society really wants. In December 2020, the **Jupiter/Saturn conjunction in Aquarius** moves onto the ascendant of China. **Pluto** moves into this territory in 2024. We, above all, need leadership that is intelligent, calm, sane, and willing to acknowledge territorial boundaries. China will continue to be on the rise; however, it will be a bumpy ride. The severe pollution of their air and waterways, their enormous sovereign debt since they built a city that is unoccupied, and financed the beginning of the "New Silk Road" that is not profitable (their credit rating was recently lowered for the first time in 25 years), and their government's autocratic rule will all present serious issues that they will need to confront.

A future in which we are no longer involved in conflicts with nations solely to stabilize the price of oil and engage ourselves in ethnic/civil wars in the Middle East, or territory in the South China Sea would be a future we could believe in. The development of sustainable energy to replace fossil fuels will revolutionize our economies and our world.

The Terrible Truth

The terrible truth at this point is that without broad access to enormous amounts of energy we would plunge backward into the Stone Age. This is the "pitch" of the oil barons. Here in the U.S., fracking, a technology for drilling into shale to acquire oil and gas deposits supposedly to make us "energy independent" presents a reality that contains severe pollution of our air and aquifers and earthquake activity where none existed before. The consequences of all this are looming. Economies will be troubled and war may be in the picture again in the 2020s. **Pluto goes into Aquarius** in 2024. **Neptune goes into Aries** in 2025, and **Uranus goes into Gemini** in 2026. The previous periods when **Uranus went into Gemini** were the American Revolution, the Civil War, and World War II. The key drivers during these periods were: disruption of established governments, breakthrough technologies, and major wars significant to American history. The rise of China into a major world power, competing for markets and resources with the U.S. and the E.U. is well on its way now. Will history repeat itself? How serious this may be is yet to be determined.

The "dark side" of all this has resulted in the accumulation by multiple nations of massive sovereign wealth debt and environmental pollution that will affect the future of all nations. Over the past 25 years we have forged trade agreements with "emerging" nations such as Mexico, Brazil, China, and India. Economic growth took off in these nations without looking at risks and consequences. Venezuela, a petroleum-dependent nation has an economy that has crashed and its government has been taken over by a dictator. Brazil impeached its prime minister last year and is impeaching its present one now for massive corruption as its petroleum-dependent economy is highly unstable. They have cut down over half of their rain forests and their environment is literally swimming in pollution. As referred to above, China has had their credit rating lowered for the first time in 25 years and is deeply in debt for financing a huge modern city that nobody occupies and a "New Silk Road" train system that makes no profits. Their environment is so contaminated that people frequently wear masks while walking outdoors in their cities. India, also suffering severe pollution of their air and waterways, has incurred massive debts as well and their development of software billionaires has not helped the millions of tribal lower classes that still live in abject poverty. To their credit, they have recently installed massive solar arrays to move to sustainable energies.

World trade is a great idea, but not when it benefits a few at the "top of the food chain" and makes the lives of most of the human population miserable. The coming transits in **Aquarius** will likely turn this tide toward the need to benefit the people-at-large. The United States will no longer be the single super power. China, currently a Communist dictatorship, will be extending its influence throughout Asia and beyond. Europe is increasingly distancing itself from America. The European Union has a financial tsunami ahead with Greece, Italy, Spain, and Portugal unable to pay their debts.

A Crisis of Confidence

A 2017 Edelman Trust Barometer study revealed the largest ever-recorded drop in trust for institutions, including government, business, media, and non-government organizations. It was reported that trust in business fell 52% in 18 countries and CEO trust also fell globally. Democratic republics, including our own United States, are experiencing chaos and conflict. The U.S. dollar is falling and is losing its status as the reigning global currency. All current systems will be shifting and reinventing themselves. The planetary configurations suggest we will have a global economic crisis, leading to a series of ideological movements toward change. Some refer to this as the "Great Reset." The establishment will become disestablished!

What lies ahead?

In December 2020, as I stated above, there is a **conjunction of Jupiter and Saturn in the sign of Aquarius**, heralding a twenty-year cycle that will likely be the beginning of a change in the entire economic paradigm. The last time this astrological event in this sign occurred was in 1405, arguably a point at which societies were moving from the Middle Ages into the Renaissance in Europe. The difference now is that global economies and the natural environment on the planet as-a-whole are at stake. Human use of fossil fuels has disturbed the global climate, resulting in extinctions of life that have not been seen since the dinosaurs disappeared. The National Oceanic and Atmospheric Association (NOAA) recently reported the highest concentration of CO2 in the air in 800,000 years! Nuclear fission energy production has resulted in catastrophes at Chernobyl in Russia and Fukushima in Japan. Currently, new nuclear fission plants are being built all over Asia, while hundreds of plants and their sites are leaking and decaying here in the U.S. and throughout the globe, and we cannot put the nuclear genie back into the bottle. In my opinion, this **conjunction in Aquarius** (a futuristic sign of genius and technology) symbolizes the potential for the end of the age of fossil fuels. We may invent our way out of this crisis with the advent of nuclear fusion, expansive solar and wind energy, passive housing architecture, and a "perfect battery" for storage. Since the **Pluto in Aquarius** will be transiting the Ascendant of the chart of China, this nation could be a leader in these technologies and benefit in world trade. I will discuss this in more detail in ensuing chapters.

The hope is that this directional change could evoke a significant transformation in economies, providing new jobs designing, installing, and maintaining the technologies of an energy revolution. **Uranus enters the sign of Taurus** (May 2018–April 2026), a sign whose concern is the health and stability of the earth itself. **Uranus** is a planet of innovation and suggests economies will focus on land conservation and a truly viable "green revolution." Instead of capitulating to the dominance of a monopoly of industrialized farming that depletes soil and water, poisons life with the use of weed killers and insecticides, we may organize local organic farms and gardens surrounding towns and cities designed to healthfully feed themselves. We may plant millions of carbon-absorbing trees, even in terraces located on tall buildings and replace the devastated rain forests. We may discover that "small is better" as grass roots local worker-owned entrepreneurship gains strength, replacing many giant stores with their transnational means of production. All of this could fuel a rush to "re-localize" away from sprawling suburbs into "green" cities to conserve land and civic resources containing "smart" infrastructures.

We may see the re-emergence of the notion of a "balance of power" between government and business. Importantly, more people may discover that they would be better served to train themselves as entrepreneurs rather than as employees. Small innovative, creative businesses lie at the heart of successful economies. New careers involving studies and services in genetic analysis, engineering, and counseling will be growing as breakthroughs in medical research will revolutionize the health field. Robotics, electrical engineering, environmental science, and physics will be excellent choices for young people today.

Because environmental and climate emergencies will have expressed themselves to the point we can no longer ignore them, there will be movements **AWAY FROM COASTAL REGIONS AROUND THE WORLD, INLAND TO PLACES OF ELEVATION SURROUNDED BY FARMLAND AND SOURCES OF FRESH WATER**. Economies will be more localized out of necessity. Global trade agreements will not go away but will be re-examined as to their viability. The U.S. will still be engaged in regional conflicts as to the role of the central government vs. local governments and the part they play in local economies. Both political parties will be so damaged that they will have to evolve or will disappear. Constitutional changes will likely be proposed and the power of the presidency will be questioned.

New Safety Nets

The proposals involving single-payer health insurance for all and an "income for life" that would replace social security, unemployment insurance, and disability insurance are being discussed and examined as we speak, with the recognition that secure long-term employment for most people is not likely to work in this era. We are already in a crisis connected to health insurance in the U.S., and the current legislature is making it worse rather than better. Many of these social programs have been successfully in place for many years in Scandinavian countries and successfully control medical costs. A broad "safety net" may be necessary to prevent mass displacement, poverty, and the ensuing spread of disease and crime that accompanies failed economies. We may feel the need to restore regulations for food, pharmaceutical, and environmental industries. Deregulated big "pharma" has been producing and selling opioid pain killers for years with little government oversight. We now have an opioid and heroin epidemic that is the worst in our history. We have an aging and less healthy population whose needs will have to be addressed. The "balance" needs to be restored.

The issue of "workers' rights" is hard to address in a society that needs very few workers. When there are hundreds of people applying for a job, people tend to accept what a company offers with no negotiation. Unions have been effective in the past, and have lost their influence in recent years; but, without them, teachers and construction workers would all be making minimum wage and no companies would be providing health insurance. We need to come to terms with what is a fair wage, adjusted to the cost of living. Headlines tell us that corporations cannot "fill" the jobs that are needed. What these headlines do not tell us is that corporations no longer invest in "training" their workers, expecting that they will walk in the door knowing their highly specialized applications. Many small businesses are forced to offer low wages or "temporary" jobs because the cost of providing health insurance to their employees is so high. The Devil is in the Details!

Immigration has been a hot topic and a big platform for political debates. Our economy would be "hollowed out" without immigrants who work hard and frequently establish small successful entrepreneurial enterprises. We need to remember that all who currently live in the U.S., except Native Americans, are from immigrant families. Yet, bringing in immigrants who will work at bottom-feeding wages and firing citizens has proven to be unacceptable. The system needs reform and it has not happened. It will happen, in my opinion, in the 2020s.

Good Investments

Due to human-induced climate change, fresh potable water supplies are diminishing globally. For those who want to invest, the area of water purification and conservation technology is a good place to go. We are in the midst of a giant real estate "bubble" that is beginning a decline in high-end areas in the U.S. and Canada. This is going to be trending down very soon. If you wait until the bottom of the real estate market is reached in 2020, you may be able to purchase real estate for investment at a much lower price. It may be advisable to buy rich inland farmland since feeding our nation will become an increased concern. As Warren Buffet famously advised, "Sell high; buy low." The other areas, which I have recommended in my previous books are green energy (solar and windmill) and **Cyber Security**. Recently, Equifax, a credit score provider was hacked with vital information of over 143 million people in the U.S. threatened. Trail blazer, Elon Musk, has already developed Tesla successfully and other companies are now following his lead, creating electric cars. There is a project underway to construct a giant underground super train that spans our entire continent. Musk's SpaceX venture with Richard Branson is combining intelligence and resources with NASA (National Aeronautics and Space Administration) to bring into reality the goal of long-term space travel for humans in the future. Bio-genetic engineering will surge in the 2020s. Robotics industries will be "unstoppable." I will refer to this in later chapters. As is being discussed now in Washington, giant infrastructure projects across our nation would provide employment and improve the standard of living for all.

Oceans rising and flooding, the increase in mega-hurricanes, many areas suffering severe drought and famine will bring on even more mass migrations out of areas that populations can no longer survive. As I stated above, people will increasingly be forced to move inland away from coastal regions, inland, to places where there is abundant fresh water and farmland. Businesses in real estate in "safe zones," passive architecture, and civic and municipal planning will be taking off in the 2020s.

Japan has been a major trading partner and ally of the U.S. since the end of World War II. Sadly, their astrological chart points to major crises in this nation with their banking system, population demographics, and the environment. **Pluto, Saturn, and Jupiter will collide in a conjunction** between 2018 and 2020, suggesting economic and environmental upheavals to come that will affect the Japanese economy since they own a substantial amount of U.S. Treasury bonds.

The rise of "digital" currency

The recent rise of Bitcoin, an online digital currency, referred to as "blockchain," is being observed as a test for something much broader and greater. The Chinese have been the largest investors, but it is rumored that China may soon outlaw this market. However, more importantly, people are using their smart phones and computers not only to buy products and transfer balances, but are now engaging in what is referred to as "remote lending." Mortgages and business loans are now being transacted online all over the world as information about borrowers is now available on the internet. It is only a matter of time before a movement to eliminate private cash transactions will be leading the public-at-large into a quagmire never seen before, instituting a global digital currency. Some refer to this as the creation of "Fed Coin" that may be created without the traditional "backing." It is suggested that the powers-that-be would not, at first, eliminate cash – they would simply stop printing it, so that fewer and fewer people would be able to use it. We are already plagued with massive hacking and millions of people have been affected whose identity has been stolen, along with their money. In addition, a person may be vulnerable to having his/her accounts erased from existence if the "powers that be," for whatever reason, do not "like" that individual.

Questions will rise. Do you wish to be under the financial control of the giant banks and lending institutions? Do you want to give up your ability to protect yourself from financial disasters by holding cash and gold privately? Do you wish to make yourself vulnerable to being "erased" economically? The "dark side" of **Aquarius**, the sign of grand innovation, brings to our attention the equally grand "Frankenstein Factor"- innovation without looking at the consequences.

Alternatives

Another, even more profound change may take place, and that is the emergence of an economic model quite different from the monopoly capitalism that will have climaxed under the **Pluto/Saturn conjunction in Capricorn** of January 2020. **Aquarius** is a sign concerned with the return of the democratic ideals of the American Revolution – a government by and for the people and a "free market" economy that opens doors for all those who are willing to work for it. We must never forget, however, that the historic exceptions to these delegated powers and economic privileges were women, Native Americans, and African slaves. We have come a long way, and yet still suffer from what the famous novel, *Animal Farm* (George Orwell, 1945), states: "Some people are more equal than others." Our societies may revisit the origin of these ideals and what it will take for them to evolve and manifest into the future, as **Pluto enters the sign of Aquarius** in 2024.

We may address the need for a balance of power between government and enterprise. In order for this to happen, the people at large have to *wake up* and pay attention to important issues and where candidates really stand. They need to vote and demand their voting rights. **Pluto** was last present in that sign when the U.S. won the Revolutionary War and at the time of the French Revolution. In the U.S. the "power of the presidency" will come into question as well as an examination of corruption in the legislatures. Hopefully, LEADERSHIP will emerge that has integrity, honesty, and intelligence, and people will be able to recognize and discern who these people really are. Is the price of liberty death, or the reward of a life well lived? Get ready for "earth shaking" changes. Questions emerge.

Will we wind up with a hoard of "mad scientists" that replace ourselves with robots that move into great wars that use massively destructive weapons, and that wipe out most life on earth? Will we invent our way out of the energy crisis, form economies that work well for most people that are "crowd funded" entrepreneurial enterprises that are worker-owned and less hierarchical? Will we create less "centralized" economies around local organic farming, water purification and effective infrastructure management, green energy, the "vocational trades," passive housing architecture, and a sharing mentality that could increase the quality of life itself? Will people be educated enough, awake enough, determined enough able to take charge of their own fate?

Choices will be made!

Chapter 4

● ● ●

Information Choices

❖ The Analyst

The Information Revolution is the pivotal mechanism of our continuing evolution.

*"Those who know do not speak. Those
who speak do not know."*

LAO TZU

Economic decisions are the #1 influence on extinction/evolution challenges. Economic choices are based on a combination of goals and the informaion available at the time. That's the problem today. There is now too much information, changing too fast, and with little or no control over the content or the ability to identify the most accurate and useful inputs. Perhaps the most serious abuse of information today, which ripples out to every other activity, is the complete breakdown of political information. We correctly worry about the ability of humans to manage nuclear weapons, medical epidemics, and artificial intelligence of the future, but the reality is that we already have fallen behind in our ability to manage information creation, distribution, interpretation, and application.

Trends, challenges, actions, and opportunities

* We use the words information and data generically, but the actual culprit is the information "content," with its message, intention, emotion, and psychology. There is a famous line from Shakespeare: *"…for there is nothing either good or bad, but thinking makes it so," (Hamlet, Act 2, Scene 2).* We can apply this idea to information with this adaptation of that quote: "Information is neither good nor bad, but intention makes it so."

* Information overload and content abuse, along with their intended and unintended consequences will get worse, not better, in the coming years. The current trend is quite clear — information is now controlled by relatively few companies, political parties, and economic entities.

* Information expertise is both an art and science, and the greatest efforts are being made by entities who try to use information as propaganda for specific political, ideological, and economic objectives, and not necessarily for the greater good.

* Future opportunities will be in the commercial development of simplified and widespread use of processes for information selection, distillation, and vetting capabilities at the individual and institutional level. Sophisticated information systems and database designs are already established, e.g., artificial intelligence, predictive analytics, relational databases, interactive query, and Watson-like programs. Collecting and sorting information and data is easy; **but the systematic ability to determine accuracy and the highest value and benefit applications is in its very infancy.**

> *"Unfortunately, we now live in an age*
> *where opinion is considered*
> *a substitute for facts."*
>
> (AUTHOR UNKNOWN)

"Data is not information, information is not knowledge, knowledge is not understanding, understanding is not wisdom."

CLIFFORD STOLL

How did information influence get to its present state?

There have been five major stages of "information influence" throughout history:

1. **Before books**. Before the printing press, information was exclusively in human memory/oral history and very limited records controlled by churches and rulers.

2. **Printing.** Printed materials expanded the diversity, quantity, and distribution of information for the next several hundred years. Information creation was still relatively slow and the content was long-lasting.

3. **Electronic communications of the 20th century.** These communications include the telephone, radio, and television, mass media, the proverbial quantum leap in quantity, diversity, speed of distribution, and access. During the early years there was a reasonable level of content discipline and some censorship. As cable systems matured, there was an expansion of content diversity and loss of control, and the first signs of information overload and abuse.

4. **Computer age.** Computers were originally tools to collect and analyze vast amounts of information that would not be practical with manual methods. Then the first generation of computer-based communications arrived in the blink of an eye, i.e., "We've got mail."

5. **Modern Internet.** The Internet changed everything about data and information and presented unlimited, uncontrolled information.

An inventory of information challenges

Fortunately, most information/data systems that operate in our daily lives in the United States and most countries employ reasonable controls, documentation, and reporting that enable an orderly and a relatively safe life. In health care, food safety, financial services, industrial operations, and aircraft operations there are efficient and widespread information procedures.

However, information about ideas is one of the core extinction/evolution challenges. We want to focus on the macro-level challenges. Here are my top ten information challenges to the choices we need to make for the greater good.

1. Something we don't even know about now. It is inevitable that there is another threat incubating, and it is difficult to prepare for what we don't know. But we can work on what we do know.

2. Intentionally fake/false/made-up information does not help/serve any issue.

3. "Cherry picking" means choosing selective elements presented as complete or sufficient to serve a purpose, but typically can distort the full context.

4. "False equivalency" is one of the most pernicious information abuses today. Upon first hearing, many comparisons seem reasonable - the familiar "two sides to every story." But most false equivalency statements are not equivalent; they are intended to dismiss legitimate inequalities.

5. Credibility/Credentials/Intention of the information provider is more important than ever. Everyone can be an "expert" with just an opinion.

6. Incomplete/Missing necessary data can cloud the issues for use by others.

7. There is too much information for others to know, find, and absorb. They often don't even know it exists.

8. Information can be too fast and too changeable, so people can't keep up.
9. Information can be too late and, therefore, not timely enough to use.
10. Information is not accessible; it is often restricted, protected, or hidden from use.

Hyper-information and its primary delivery systems of 24/7 news have become the dominant influence on beliefs, expectations, preferences, prejudices, and behavior. The new combinations of the disparate information are a new force of influence. We have news and information which emerge and expand every minute of every day and every single person in the world can be a content creator.

We are in perpetual information bubbles overwhelmed with inadequate tools to manage what we read and hear. Information/News has become a primary weapon of economic, social, cultural, religious, and environmental conflicts.

Most news has a short shelf life from a couple of days to a few weeks. But we often make decisions too quickly, pressured by the flow of new information. We cannot stop making decisions because the information changes so frequently, but we can avoid knee-jerk responses.

* Look at the near-term trends of three months. The biggest stories have a life expectancy of just a few weeks. It is not that a situation disappears, such as a natural disaster, but today's big story is replaced by another big story in a few weeks. Even in political campaigns that run for months or years, specifics of stories change with incredible speed. Be more aware of the mini-cycles within the overall cycles. Include astrological assessments that apply to the scope of your decision and planning timing.

Astrology offers contextual and cyclical guidance about the conditions that might favor or be a detriment to specific kinds of decisions. The ways in which we make choices are no longer operating adequately to assure survival in a complex environment dominated by fallible information. But the tools to employ new choice/decision methods are available. *Astrology provides what we have been talking about, "information," that has been documented and connected to observable events over several thousand years of history. There is no other information discipline with that type of pedigree.*

Information is about content and there are endless possibilities and opportunities.

Four macro-level information challenges are included below:

1. **Within the next eight to ten years there will be an information privacy crisis beyond what we have already encountered.** We have had *WikiLeaks*, persistent hacking of confidential sites, cyber security intrusions and pervasive fake news. We already cannot trust information received from many critical sources. Fake information about infrastructure, healthcare, transportation, financial transactions, and, of course, politics, all have extraordinarily negative consequences.

2. **There will be an unstoppable move to create institutional levels of information privacy, accuracy assessment, and legitimacy filters**. The movie, *"Minority Report,"* (Spielberg, deCont, Molen, Parkes, & Curtis, 2002), starring Tom Cruise, was based on a book by science fiction great, Philip K. Dick. The movie told the story about the government's ability to screen human thoughts to preemptively identify potential criminal activities before they became a reality and to intervene as soon as possible. Reading human thoughts and intentions may be fantasy, but there will be analogous programs to curb information content flow to minimize the chance for harmful/destructive information to be disseminated, let alone acted upon. Algorithms will be developed to identify and match information sources, recipients, content, and implications. Free speech is necessary, but technology requires new definitions

of the boundaries of free speech about intentional deception and harm. The simplest tools we have today are credit monitoring and security services that monitor basic activity to alert and take actions to alert or stop harmful activity. There will be a new system of information monitoring, customized to specific business and social sectors. As we write this book, in September 2017, *Facebook* has already announced they are hiring thousands of people to provide direct oversight of content to help reduce the abuses of the system.

3. **Financial markets will absolutely need new measures of information relevant to risk and relativity to remain viable.** Fundamental data about company sales and profits are a given, but right now the entire industry is built on expectations, hypotheticals, and probabilities. The hyper-information financial markets had a good run. But the next major crash will mandate change in financial services and structure. Just as Las Vegas gambling machines were once manipulated to favor the house before they became regulated with technical controls – the same is likely to happen in the financial markets. Financial/Investment/Information will have to include more user-friendly and detailed "list of ingredients" that go beyond the current historical data and future performance disclaimers. New specifications will include reader-friendly statistics about the level of speculation or risk with more specificity. But this is a more complex and ambiguous issue for another time.

4. **For the foreseeable future, markets will be totally dominated by uncertainty and volatility.** Uncertainty is largely a manufactured byproduct of existing knowledge - we know the Federal Reserve will do something but we don't know when or to what extent. The volatility in markets is the quantitative reaction to new information received today and it is different from the information we used yesterday. Thus, the level of volatility is a mirror of the level of uncertainty and the inadequate information available that precedes decisions. We have learned that with instant and pervasive communications come instant, unpredictable information. From

my own macro-trend analytics research over the past 15 years, there are a couple of generalizations I have discovered:

* Information has a shelf life of four to six weeks before the next major event dominates the news. Some news lasts only one day or two days.

* My research shows that economic and political news take about two weeks to stabilize and yield a useful set of information to use in your decisions. The nature of volatility we see daily is the proverbial knee-jerk reaction to the latest news, without fully accommodating the fact that tomorrow it will change once again.

The two great forces in the world today are politics and economics, and they are intimately intertwined.

* As we have seen in the past few election cycles, and most significantly in 2016, politics is now a matter of mastery of information and news. Information no longer must be accurate; its sole purpose among practitioners is to stimulate an emotional response that is favorable to the provider.

* As a call to action, the 2016 election was better than any fiction writer could conceive. Every type of communication vehicle, absence of adequate verification and fact checking, intervention by foreign sources, and the seeming inability of the forces of good to know how to fight back with equal measures of information. If any good is to come from the 2016 election, it will be the awakening of people to the need to be more informed and the will to develop new processes to reduce the abuse of political news and rhetoric. And perhaps most of all, more people must vote. The apathy of nearly 40% of the population is a bigger threat than the misinformed.

* It is extraordinary that we have regulations and standards on food labeling, truth in advertising, and 20 pages of the dangers of taking a medicine. Companies that fail to adhere to the information rules

can be severely punished. If a company CEO makes a derogatory statement, if a newscaster makes a bad joke about ethnicity, they are rebuked or fired.

* But the words that come from the mouths of politicians seem to have no constraints for rules because we, the people, have not sufficiently demanded these rules. We would like to believe that recent events will prompt actions to bring greater truth in politics into modern times. If we are wrong, the U.S. democracy will turn a corner and retreat to some type of government we won't recognize. And in the U.S., unfortunately, politics has become too much of an entertainment.

* But history is very clear — every political society and civilization had its own cycles and everyone reached a peak and then fell back to a lower level. We don't know how things will turn out in the United States yet, but the potential for a retreat of our democratic political system in the U.S. is very possible.

My forecast is that the United States is at the cusp of a major realignment of political structures, parties, and values, but conflicts will not be resolved anytime soon. And as U.S. politics are more confused internally and in their relations with other nations, the U.S. is poised to lose more stature and leadership throughout the world.

* U.S. weakness is ripe for exploitation by other major powers - China, Russia, and to a lesser extent, Western Europe. All have a stake in the global economy, control of strategic resources, and political influence. The only barrier to the U.S. loss of power is an even greater retreat in China and or Europe. The U.S. is still the best "haven," but this honor by default is not in our survival interest.

* Within the next two to three presidential election cycles, the nature of the U.S. political system could evolve for the better. The current faux populism might evolve to a more representative populism, ala

Bernie Sanders. Or, there will be continued consolidation of power and economics in the minority.

*   The conventional recommendation is for individuals to be more involved and more informed and discerning about news. We agree, but it will never happen at a level sufficient to stop current information abuse. There is too much information, and we, as individuals, do not have the time or skills to verify all the information we encounter. Thus, the nascent efforts of *Facebook, Twitter* and other communications platforms can provide the first-level filters to accuracy and potential dangerous intent. There is a fine line between freedom of speech and censorship, but over the last few years we have seen the damage runaway information can inflict. New rules are necessary to deal with threats that did not exist when the free speech concepts were created.

• • •

❖ The Astrologer

The 20th century brought us into an age of communication and information sharing that has been as revolutionary as the invention of the printing press. Radio, telephone, television, computers, the Internet, and smart phones all have established lines of communication and informed literally billions of people in the developed world. The **Uranus/Neptune conjunction** (innovation plus expansion) **in Capricorn** in 1993 and the ensuing **transits of Uranus and Neptune in Aquarius** have led us to characterize this age as the Second Industrial Revolution or, as many say, the Information Age. People who possess this technology have access to all this 24 hours a day, seven days a week.

Many of us who are in the "senior" category are struck by how many young people are literally buried in their laptops and smart phones – walking down the street texting, tweeting, chatting, and barely looking up to see if they are in oncoming traffic! Others of us are constantly complaining how "dumbed down" television has become and are confused amidst the hundreds of channels, recorded, and "live streaming" on our computers, throwing more choices into the mix. There are brilliant dramas, great concerts, sports of every kind, nature and science series – a veritable cornucopia of possibilities from which we may choose. However, as with all human pursuits, there is a "dark side" to the availability of so many channels and online sites. We have been confronted with online pornography, prostitution and human trafficking, gambling, internet "bullying," sites that promote destructive and dangerous cults, and an array of evils that lie at the bottom of the human psyche waiting to emerge. People are becoming more digital and less personally interactive with each other and the natural world around them. Buried in their remote devices, there is no time for critical thinking or contemplation that leads to more positive human traits such as compassion, empathy, inspiration, and expanded creative intelligence.

Although there are documentaries, dramas, educational and news programs of quality, most frequently on PBS (Public Broadcasting Service), standards for reporting have precipitately fallen and many news channels have taken political positions and become shouting matches instead of venues for intelligent debates. In 1987, laws in the U.S. demanding that news stations comply with a standard of quality and accuracy were taken off the books. We can see the result and that is we are literally drowning in information and starving for truth, insight, and quality. Some might refer to all this as the "Age of Information Pollution." Behind all this is a media that, as a whole, is run by giant corporations that are primarily interested in ratings, promoting their agendas, and profits from their sponsors. There are courageous, truth-telling journalists, but they are, too often, criticized or marginalized out of the mainstream. Media industries are becoming monopolies. *Fox News, The Wall Street Journal,* and *USA Today* are all owned by Rupert Murdoch. Sinclair Broadcast Group is on the verge of acquiring the *Tribune Media* (42 TV stations) that would result in Sinclair reaching 72 percent of the country.

Whatever happened to education?

For many years, the U.S. has enjoyed status in the world as having the finest colleges and universities. In recent years, these institutions of higher learning have been run like corporations interested in "profits-only" bottom line, cheap labor, and a movement of money into the pockets of the top brass. The cost of college has risen through the stratosphere and the availability of government loans to students has indebted an entire generation to spending many years of their lives paying off their loans. Meanwhile, according to published scores on international achievement examinations, the quality of public education has declined in the U.S. while other nations like Singapore, Taiwan, Denmark, Norway, Sweden, Finland, Germany, and France move upward. How we receive information, the cost of an education, where we put our priorities at this point in time is primarily run by corporate America. Federally financed programs for the public schools are being systematically eliminated. Local property taxes pay for the public schools that are losing their financing in low income neighborhoods throughout the nation. Families with considerable financial means are sending their children to high-end expensive private schools. Parents and teachers alike are desperate for solutions and improvements. There is an ongoing conflict with respect to charter schools and private schools of all types, the issue of "school choice," and the defunding of public institutions. All of this is tied in with the economic choices we have made as a nation and as a culture. Economics, information, and technology are all tied in together.

A matter of supreme importance in U.S. education is the removal of civics, political science, and history from many of the high schools. Children have little or no knowledge of the constitution, the rule of law, and the workings of our system of governance. A democratic republic such as ours will fail unless the public has this crucial understanding of how the system works. Former Supreme Court Justice, Sandra Day O'Conner, has been on a campaign to reinstitute these courses back into the schools in recent years.

Some positive actions have taken place. Online colleges and universities are emerging as excellent choices for an advanced education that are less costly and more convenient, especially for working students. Online libraries like *Wikipedia* are a source of information with a swath so wide and all-encompassing that they are like having our own personal library. We can go to science publications, weather sites, medical information sites, and *Google* nearly everything. Online newsletters, especially the not-for-profit ones, often present essays and editorials of high quality, rescuing us from brain oblivion. We can express our views and ideas on our websites, through social media, and email one another about anything. Many highly successful businesses are online enterprises.

The looming questions remain. Who controls the information? Is all this information enlightening us? Is it encouraging critical thinking and analysis? Is it inspiring us to be creative and insightful?

What Next?

The massive upheavals that lie ahead between 2018 and 2027 will be less about the next "great" smartphone or tweeting account and more about our losing trust and confidence in our institutions and our willingness to make intelligent and informed changes to these structures. We may examine the need to give concerted thought to a society that could move its "message" from the "Age of Quantity" (accumulating vast amounts of wealth and property at any cost), to the "Age of Quality" (prosperity in economies and improved societies that lend purpose and inspiration to our lives). As **planets move into Aquarius** (innovation, humanitarianism, and mass consciousness), the long reign of "mechanistic materialism" as the only way of life will come into question. I will explore this idea in later chapters. Meanwhile, in the near future, I see a growing division between "haves" and "have-nots" not only connected to economics, but connected to the ability to evaluate information using intellectual discrimination, and promoting healthy questioning as opposed to the current emphasis on opinionated fear mongering. To close this gap will be one of the great challenges lying ahead.

The availability of quality information and intelligent debate lies at the heart of a democratic society's success. The **Aquarian Age** will demand advancing and ongoing education throughout our lives. I also see a new direction in curricula for students and their studies. Rather than emphasizing training people to be employees, our education system could train people to be innovators and entrepreneurs and provide information about what it takes to create a successful business ranging from one in the vocational trades, to technology, to finance, to communication, to the arts, etc. Because this **Aquarian period** highlights effective "group think" and organizations of friends, people could put together businesses with friends as their partners in these enterprises. Training and information will likely become more available to those pursuing these pathways. Studies by educators for many years support that classes in the fine arts, daily exercise, and communication, are as important as mathematics and science. All subjects need to address each student's emotional responses and the need for creative self-expression as opposed to a linear, machine-like, test-directed approach to teaching children.

We may ask ourselves how we can create economies and an environment that work for us and that do not ask us to sacrifice our sanity and health for jobs that are stultifying and for companies that are using us as "commodities" that are disposable. We might re-envision both management and employees participating in an atmosphere of innovation and creativity that benefits all of us. This depends upon the quality of information that is available to us and our ability and willingness to access and survey it with open minds.

In the coming **Age of Aquarius,** it is up to us whether we embrace the fate of being "the Sheeple" or claim the rights and privileges of being "the People." Mass communication that appeals to the "herd" mentality is an ever-present danger that threatens people's willingness and ability to make conscious decisions and take personal responsibility for them.

The choice is ours!

Chapter 5

● ● ●

Technology Choices

❖ The Analyst

Technology could be defined as a vast harnessing of scientific principles to produce products and processes of benefit to end-users. In our wise-choice world, technology decisions would be based on outcomes that do the greatest good, but that is not the reality.

There is scientific innovation for the sake of science, natural curiosity, and the need to learn and build upon past knowledge. In this book, we want to recognize the potential of technology to address our challenges and reprioritize the economics of resource allocation.

We will focus on three aspects that are directly related to our extinction/evolution issues:

1. Technology philosophies.
2. Energy solutions.
3. Environmental solutions.

Trends, challenges, actions, opportunities

* There will always be the pursuit of the scientific, but as of 2017, the political will is somewhere between disinterested and anti-scientific

investment, which will thwart both needed solutions and U.S. leadership in these sectors.

* Investment in technology is driven more by potential market size and Return on Investment (ROI) than by extinction/evolution benefits.
* Within ten years there will be a consolidation of scientific/technological collaboration to work on the extinction/evolution conditions. The collaboration will be forced by the increased urgency of environmental change, an economic disparity revolution, and the inevitable unintended consequences of current activities.
* Technology that does not require enormous investments, such as software, process management, information technology, and similar low labor/low capital resources will thrive. Venture capital has been mesmerized by legitimate but not high-priority survival metrics, including:
  * Leverage - small investments yield big absolute and relative returns.
  * "Eyeballs"– massive audiences have monetary continuity for investors.

  Investments in leverage/eyeball technology do provide some efficiencies and short-term returns, but not survival benefits.
* Fiscal policies offer the best use of tax reform on the corporate side in support for technology and infrastructure development and related job creation.

Technology Choices

Technology has been a marvel of human evolution and provided extraordinary improvements in life. But today we are at the crossroads of determining how to use technology for the greatest good and as a remedy against potential extinction of our way of life. Many technologies have evolved faster than the human ability to use them safely and most effectively. We need to reset technological priorities to the current threats. With a bit of planning, consensus, and wisdom, technology prioritization can be both beneficial and still financially successful to businesses.

The inevitable questions include both the "who" and the "how" of priority setting. We do not have years for debate, and there is no single authority to mandate the priorities. I think most vested interests do understand the nature of the challenges and what is most practical to begin. To help start the discussion, we have created our scorecard of technology needs and priorities.

We have considered the absolute need, feasibility, and ultimate benefit and rate each technology on five criteria presented in the chart below. We have used a ranking of 1 – 10, with 10 being the "most" and 1 being the "least." Thus, energy is ranked 10 as being the most critical technological need, and artificial intelligence is a 5, a less important need. Similarly, energy ranks 8 for time to deliver, meaning that it takes a relatively long time, whereas information security technologies are ranked at 3, requiring relatively little time to develop and deploy.

Our ranking criteria are the following:

* **Absolute need**: New systems and remedies to current threats are critical.
* **Resource intensity**: The level of material and financial resources needed to develop and deploy.
* **Time to deliver**: The time needed to implement the technology on a meaningful scale.
* **Economic Benefits**: These benefits include the net economic growth, jobs, wages, cost efficiency, and ROI.
* **Importance in our extinction/evolution context**: Is this of benefit to the people at large and the health of the planet?

Technology Relevant Choices and Priorities						
Target	Need	Resource intensity	Time to implement	Economic benefit	Extinction Evolution benefit	Comment
Information, cyber security	10	5	3	10	10	Active threat to all challenges
Energy	10	10	8	10	10	Core cost, survival resource
Environmental	10	7	6	10	10	Basic survival
Education	8	5	4	8	7	Need skills for all issues
Infrastructure	7	8	7	8	6	Need physical resources
Communications	7	3	3	6	5	Core mechanism of all activities
Transportation	6	6	6	7	4	Need for access, distribution
AI, analytics	5	4	3	5	3	More R&D, discovery
Healthcare	5	4	5	6	5	A "right", but not critical to immediate challenges

Source: 3iconexxion research www.3imacroanalytics.com

Technology has constraints as well as saturation. Technological investment can add features and efficiency but not necessarily expand the total market. Innovation in consumer technologies is only increasing minimally in the relative scheme of things. For example, a laptop that can separate and work as a tablet is a great convenience, maybe even fun, but it is not a driver of incremental growth. And the feature vs. value of new technologies is becoming increasingly thin. There is always a market for incremental gains, but these do not drive macro-growth. Many high-profile economic choices are for the communications environment. For example, the economics of social media is based on two things: more users and advertising revenue. But the advertising/commercial revenue base has a diminishing return curve since there is a finite capacity to expand marketing expenses and advertising revenues unless accompanied by an increase in audience buying, and that is also finite.

There could be a next generation of global equivalents to the U. S. National Institutes of Health (NIH) and National Science Foundation (NSF). Science and academia do collaborate extensively, but our guess is that collaborative efficiency is low, well under 50%. That is, 50% or more of the effort and investment in technological development may be redundant, out-of-date, unknown, or counterproductive, and driven primarily by ROI and not by longer-term net benefit.

• • •

❖ The Astrologer

Through the ages, the human presence on planet Earth has distinguished itself from all other species by innovating and developing tools and technologies - from our designing clubs and arrows, to the discovery and harnessing of fire, the invention of the wheel, the agricultural revolution, to the so-called Stone Age and architecture, the Bronze Age, the Iron Age, the Industrial Revolution, and the discovery of oil and gas to fuel it. Since the advent of Einstein's Theory of Relativity and the discoveries of the quantum theorists leading to the splitting of the atom, (we split the atom in the 1930s when the planet **Pluto was discovered and named),** we have been in what many call the Nuclear Age, the Space Age, the Digital Age, all preceded by the development of the microscope and modern medicine, telescopes and advanced astronomy, quantum physics, computers, nanotechnology, rocketry, space travel, and, unfortunately, weaponry that could end all biological life on earth. It is said by many that we have progressed faster technologically in the past 200 years than the previous 10,000!

More recently, the advent of the personal computer, the Internet, cell phones, electric and self-driving vehicles, amazing medical procedures and technologies including cloning and stem cell research, rocketry, and journeys to the Moon and Mars, all have our collective heads spinning. Our notions of what constitutes reality have been turned upside down. We are using these resultant technologies, even while most of us do not understand the languages and terminologies of these sciences that developed them, or how we got to this point. Recently, it has been announced that the National Aeronautics and Space Administration (NASA) and Johns Hopkins University are working on the so-called Dichymos project that will be able to defend earth from incoming dangerous asteroids and comets that are destined to come our way in the future.

What is Reality?

A seminal article, "The Quantum Universe," (*Scientific American*, June 2017) was written by Yasunori Nomura, a professor of physics and director of the Berkeley Center for Theoretical Physics at the University of California, Berkeley. He is also a senior faculty scientist at Lawrence Berkeley National Laboratory and a principal investigator at the University of Tokyo's Kavli Institute for the Physics and Mathematics of the Universe. Nomura writes: "Many cosmologists now accept the extraordinary idea that what seems to be the entire universe may actually be only a tiny part of a much larger structure called the multiverse. In this picture, multiple universes exist, and the rules we once assumed were basic laws of nature take different forms in each; for example, the types and properties of elementary particles may differ from one universe to another." We have already been amazed by quantum mechanics and its theories that the movement of a subatomic particle may be influenced by its observer, leading to "probability" theory. We are now working with "quantum computers" that solve problems that the human mind struggles to even understand. Nomura states that: "In other words, before any quantum system is measured, its outcome is uncertain, but afterward all subsequent measurements will find the same result as the first."

Just when we thought we had something we might understand, along comes an entirely new theory. Nomura refers to a scientist, Hugh Everett, who, in 1957, developed and published the many-worlds interpretation of quantum mechanics, even though his ideas were not favored at the time. Nomura further explains: "Everett's key insight was that the state of a quantum system reflects the state of the whole universe around it so that we must include the observer in a complete description of the measurement. In other words, we cannot consider the ball, the winds, and the hand that throws it in isolation – we must also include in the fundamental description the person who comes along to inspect its landing spot, as well as everything else in the cosmos at that time. In this picture, the quantum state after the measurement is still a superposition – not just a superposition of two landing spots but of two entire worlds"! Just as you thought reality might be within your grasp, the author states: "A human observer, being a part of nature, cannot escape from this cycle – the observer keeps splitting into many observers living in many possible parallel worlds and all are equally 'real'."

In recent years, we have "discovered" black holes and it is thought that over 80% of the universe is comprised of so-called "dark energy" and "dark matter." Chaos Theory has given birth to the Theory of Entanglement which supposes that when twin particles are separated, they continue their coordinated "spin" even if they are at opposite ends of the universe! Some proof of this has recently been published. We have substantiated the existence of the so-called "God Particle." All this would demonstrate that what we currently can "see" or "know" is a tiny portion of a very great and grand reality. Astrologers are engaged and interested in all this since, from the beginning, we see ourselves as both open to exploring and being connected to the universe.

Medical Technologies

In February 1997, astrologers observed a truly exciting combination of planetary patterns. **Mars** (action), **Jupiter** (expansion), **Saturn** (structure), and **Uranus** (innovation), all lined up in aspect to one another, especially marked by a **Jupiter/Uranus conjunction in Aquarius**. We hypothesized that a great invention or scientific breakthrough would occur and be revealed to the public at that time. Lo and behold, it was officially announced that Dolly, the sheep, had been successfully cloned! The public reaction traversed all over the spectrum of human emotion – from elation at the possibilities this might offer for curing disease to horror at the moral implications of cloning organs to replacing diseased ones, to possibly cloning an entire human being. There was a backlash here in the U.S. that made it illegal to broadly experiment with embryonic human stem cells, even if it were used to find cures for diseases such as diabetes. The results have been mixed and it has been proven to be more difficult than originally thought to transplant stem cells. Research has continued in other countries. Ironically, that same year, we saw a highly contagious bird virus, the severe acute respiratory syndrome (SARS), develop and spread in China. Scientists, by analyzing its DNA, developed a vaccine to stop what could have been a global pandemic.

In the article, "Will We Control Our Genetic Destinies"? (*Scientific American*, September 2016), Stephen S. Hall, the author, writes about the proposed experiments in gene editing of sperm cells, conducted by Dr. Kyle Orwig, a professor at the University of Pittsburgh, who currently used mice, but may soon be "used in treatments for male infertility that involve altering the genetic code of sperm cells. Such alterations would be passed down to future generations, constituting a permanent change in the human genome." Theoretically, certain harmful genes could be removed from sperm that could cause disease later. There seems to be less outrage at this "tampering" than previous experiments involving human embryos. Hall interviewed biologist Dr. George Church of Harvard Medical School to get his opinion on the ethics and public reaction to this research. Hall states: "Church sees the germline, Rubicon, being crossed because sperm do not seem to arouse the same ethical passions as embryos or even egg cells." The article quotes Henry Greely, Director of the Center for Law and the Biosciences at Stanford University as he answers the question, "Will sex become obsolescent"? Greely replies: "No, but having sex to conceive babies is likely to become at least much less common. In 20 to 40 years, we'll be able to derive eggs and sperm from stem cells, probably the parents' skin cells. This will allow easy preimplantation genetic diagnosis on a large number of embryos or easy genome modification for those who want edited embryos instead of just selected ones." I am reminded of Aldous Huxley's 20th century book, *Brave New World* (1931).

The Return of the Age of Enlightenment

The **Jupiter/Saturn conjunction in Aquarius** in 2020 and *Pluto's transit into Aquarius* in 2024, mark a return to Pluto's position in the 1700s when the U.S. and Europe "fell in love" with science. This period is referred to as the Age of Enlightenment and occupied by our founders, Thomas Jefferson and Benjamin Franklin, whose discoveries and inventions inspired America to become a leader in technology and innovation. In this 21st century era, there will be geniuses from nations all over the world, linked by our mass communication networks to create and invent solutions to problems we now recognize as necessary to the survival and prosperity of our civilization and all life on earth. The sign of **Aquarius** also points to advancements in the study of the human brain and nervous system that may lead to cures for many mental handicaps and disorders, including autism, depression, and dementia. In July 2026, **Jupiter, Uranus, Neptune, and Pluto** contact each other in such a way that: 1) a grand invention, possibly nuclear fusion may become a reality; 2) an experiment in the area of quantum mechanics may, once again, completely transform our view of reality"; 3) a successful alteration of the human genome with the rise, once again, of cloning and stem cell transplantation that works to cure some diseases; and 4) leaders with grand visions for the transformation of human societies benefiting from science may emerge from around the world. This period contains within it a set of truly grand possibilities.

The development of robotics and computers that would replace people is a hot topic and is feared, widely debated, and already happening. Yuval Harari, author of the recent book, *Homo Deus: A Brief History of Tomorrow* (2015), when interviewed on the CNN show, *GPS* (July 23, 2017), by Fareed Zakaria stated he feared a great "power shift to algorithms." Many people believe that our technology is now and will be "smarter" than humans. Science fiction novels have been written along with movies we have all seen in which robots kill and supplant their human creators. We need to remember that humans are the creators and our machines are designed to serve our needs. They will do only what we program them to do. The miracle of biological life contains within it possibilities we have only begun to explore and there is a case to be made that humans may improve themselves by incorporating robotics, which we already do for people with paralyzed limbs, and genetically engineer an end to many of the diseases that plague us. There is also a warning that we may take a detached "soul killing," overly intellectualized pathway devoid of the appreciation of the miracle of life itself. The looming question, once again, is this: "Are we using our genius to improve humankind and life on earth, or are we Dr. Frankenstein reincarnated"? Mary Shelley wrote her great tale when **Pluto was in Aquarius,** in the late 1700s.

The chart for the December 21, 2020 **conjunction of Jupiter** (expansion) **and Saturn** (organization) also contains a serious warning with its square (conflict) of **Mars** in **Aries** (war) with **Pluto** in **Capricorn** (established nations and institutions.) Underlying this warning lies the necessity of societies getting past the competitive murderous "tribalism" that results in massive wars with each other for land, waterways, and resources that have characterized human history for thousands of years. We all now know that our stashes of weapons of mass destruction combined with political leadership and power in the hands of self-absorbed, short-sighted people may be the greatest danger to humankind since we came into existence. I will never forget the Stanley Kubrick movie, *Dr. Strangelove* (1964), in which a crazy militarized leadership in the U.S. "falls in love with the bomb" and blows up the world.

Choices will be made!

Chapter 6

● ● ●

Energy Choices

❖ The Analyst

Energy is a complex issue of environment, economics, scarcity, and politics are directly connected to quality-of-life issues. As long as energy choices are based on short-term economics and global politics instead of the impact on biological life, we will not be able to harness energy for our survival choices.

Our world of energy spans wood-burning stoves to progressive work on nuclear and alternative energies. Cleaner, safer, and lower cost sustainable energy will provide more jobs, lower costs of many products, enable basic services where they were once cost prohibitive or physically not possible, and expand the overall quality of living throughout the world.

From an economically selfish perspective, significantly reduced energy costs can provide economic growth. Greatly reduced costs of production, materials, and transportation can lower costs so that conspicuous and cosmetic assumption is tolerable. For example, if the cost of a new television is sufficiently low, then the impetus for continuous but minimal innovation can fuel continuous updating by consumers. Manufacturers need continuous growth; consumers can keep a stable level of discretionary spending;

and marketers can advertise and promote ad infinitum. This scenario may not be morally desirable, but recognizes the need for the symbiotic relationship of production and consumption for the benefit of all.

Trends, challenges, actions, opportunities

* The withdrawal of the United States from the Paris climate accord will likely slow some of the short-term efforts, but we believe the rest of the world will be able to sustain current environmental progress. In fact, the U.S. withdrawal will be the catalyst for other countries to take advantage of the void and increase their efforts in alternative energy opportunities.

* The United States may well lose scientific, commercial, market, and intellectual leadership that will be filled by other countries. China, Western Europe, possibly Brazil, and the sleeper players of Saudi Arabia or other oil-rich countries can take advantage of U.S. political confusion.

* Major energy firms may be funding the politics of the climate change deniers to buy time, but they are already investing in the future they know will arrive for renewable and alternative energy sources. But, the allure of short-term profits cannot be stopped because there is a ready market. For example, shale oil and fracking may be destructive, but technologies to make them cost-effective for a ready market may be a practical business decision.

* More rigorous efficiency/nonpolluting standards and other beneficial transitions have already started and will continue where there is a low-cost, low-risk commercial opportunity. The most recent example is the relatively quick changeover from incandescent bulbs to the high-efficiency bulbs and now light-emitting diodes (LEDs). Another likely near-term candidate - more electric vehicles.

* Nuclear fission and nuclear fusion will need to be revisited and examined. Fission needs far more advanced safety and long-term disposal processes. There is a wildcard: current work on nuclear fusion has a better than even chance of a break out in the next three to five years.

* The very wealthy Middle East countries will not go quietly into the "end-of-oil" night. They have the money, necessity, patience, and low regard for Western methods. Think of this scenario: if you are incredibly wealthy because of a natural resource that will eventually come to an end, but live in the locale of endless solar energy availability, have more than enough money to fund the secret research for the most advanced solar technology, have the political ability to set priorities and control the processes, and know that the world will absolutely need your product within 20 years — what would you be doing? If the oil-rich, solar-rich countries are not engaging in such technology, they should be.

Scorecard of energy priorities
We again created a starting assessment of the needs, feasibility, and benefits of current and future energy sources. We use the scale of 0 to 10; the higher the number the more important, more effort, more benefit; the lower numbers are less important, take less effort, and have less benefit.

Energy Choices and Priorities						
Target	Need	Resource intensity	Time to implement	Economic benefit	Extinction Evolution benefit	Comment
Solar, wind, etc.	10	5	6	10	10	Tech available, need economies of scale
Biofuels	9	7	7	8	8	Perpetual raw materials
Nuclear fusion	9	10	10	10	10	Making progress
Natural gas	8	6	5	7	3	Pragmatic interim
Nuclear-current	6	8	9	8	5	Pause, major safe disposal, focsu on alternatives
Oil/drilling	5	7	5	6	0	Remains for a long time, but end inevitable
Coal	2	5	2	1	0	Gone relatively soon
Fracking	1	7	4	2	0	Mistake based on evidence so far

Source: 3iconexxion research llc. www.3imacroanalytics.com

• • •

❖ The Astrologer

Since the dawn of the Industrial Revolution, the crux of our civilization-al development has been energy. Until the middle of the 19th Century, we burned wood by cutting down giant swaths of forests and slaughtered whales for their oil, stopping just short of bringing them to extinction. Coal mining rose, oil was discovered in Pennsylvania in 1821, natural gas was discovered, electricity was harnessed, and following World War II, with the development of atomic energy, nuclear fission plants were built in the U.S. and throughout the developed world. The rest is history.

With the advent of global climate changes thought to be due to the burning of fossil fuels, we are now looking at developing energy production that is green, sustainable, and non-polluting. The terrible meltdowns at Chernobyl, Three Mile Island, and Fukushima, as well as leaks forming in nuclear fission plants throughout the world, demonstrate that this is an alternative that has lost its luster. The Japanese have not, at this point in time, been able to stop the leaks of radioactive cesium within their territory and widely into the Pacific Ocean. Germany has already announced that it is shutting down its nuclear fission plants and moving toward sustainable energy production. Unfortunately, nuclear fission plants are now being built in China and South Korea, even though the dangers of meltdowns and wide proliferation of toxic radioactivity have moved western nations away from this choice.

The article, "Tar Sands Pipeline Companies Oversee Hundreds of Oil Spills," (Tim Donaghy & Lawrence Carter, Aug 12, 2017, truth-out. com) states the following: "Statistics from the U.S Pipeline and Hazardous Materials Safety Administration (PHMSA) – obtained as part of an investigation by Greenpeace USA, shows that oil giants - TransCanada, Kinder Morgan, and Enbridge - have together suffered 373 spills over the past seven years. Of these, the agency classified 41 as 'significant' – which for crude oil means that more than 50 barrels were spilled. This includes the notorious Kalamazoo river oil spill, which polluted 36 miles of river in 2010 and only narrowly avoided contaminating Lake Michigan." None of us can forget the BP Oil disaster in the Gulf of Mexico whose effects still linger on the Louisiana coast. Most recently, we have had to face the damage Hurricane Harvey inflicted on Houston, Texas – the largest refining and petrochemical complex in the United States.

The next chapter will explore decisions we may make with respect to the environment, but energy production is at the top of the list. In the book, *Drawdown: The Most Comprehensive Plan Ever Proposed to Reverse Global Warming,* (editor, Paul Hawken, 2017) there is a list of energy production choices, how they work, and the costs to implement them. Some of them are: methane digesters, in-stream hydro, waste-to-energy, grid flexibility, energy storage utilities (batteries), energy storage (distributed), solar water, net zero buildings, and nuclear fusion, among others. One of the **looming issues** around solar and windmill solutions is that huge amounts of fossil fuel have to be burned to supply the enormous amounts of energy to manufacture them, sending more carbon into the atmosphere, defeating its purpose.

The Big Solution

I believe all these options are worth exploring, but I think the world needs a large, comprehensive, and centralized solution. The chapter in the book on hydrogen-boron fusion, although still considered experimental, would be the "Holy Grail" of energy production. It is non-polluting and theoretically could produce infinite amounts of energy. Fusion is what powers the sun and we would reproduce it here on earth. Hawken described in the book, *Drawdown...* (p. 195) that: "Hydrogen boron fusion produces three helium atoms, and a fractional portion of remaining mass converts to energy . . . a lot of energy. Atoms can make energy in two ways: divide or unite; fission or fusion. Einstein predicted that given the right conditions, mass can become energy or vice versa, and that the amount of energy contained in a tiny bit of mass, in human terms, is astounding. Hydrogen-boron fusion produces three to four times more energy per mass of fuel than nuclear fission, with virtually no waste: That means no plutonium, no radiation, no meltdowns, and no proliferation."

In the past few years, fusion ignition experiments have been developed with different approaches in Germany, France, Switzerland, and California in the United States. Northrup Grumman recently developed a portable fusion chamber. The Massachusetts Institute of Technology (MIT) solved a problem related to electrical conductivity. In *Drawdown...* (pp. 194-195), it was announced: "In June 2015, a company that had been considered a maverick because of its unorthodox approach announced it has achieved one-half of the Holy Grail, the more difficult half, nicknamed 'long enough.' The company, Tri Alpha Energy (TAE) had been secretive for most of its eighteen-year history. And for good reason: The history of fusion energy is littered with hype, fantasy, and claims that fell flat. Better to be quiet do the work and that is what TAE did. By the time of its announcement, TAE had already completed more than forty-five thousand experimental runs." In addition to all this, the author states: "By late 2017, TAE will have built the fourth reactor in its history, one large enough to achieve fusion. With their theory of 'long enough' plasma stabilization accomplished, they now have to achieve 'hot enough.' How do you create 5.4 billion degrees Fahrenheit when the sun tops out at 25.2 million Fahrenheit? According to Binderbauer, you let the plasma do it. The Large Hadron Collider in Switzerland is creating temperatures in the trillions of degrees, a thousand times what TAE requires." It is worth reading the whole chapter for a more comprehensive understanding of the future in fusion, but important for all of us to know about possibly the most important scientific breakthrough since the splitting of the atom. We are a long way from installing the infrastructure for all this to take place, but the process itself could provide good jobs for millions of people, installing and maintaining the new theoretically limitless energy network.

I also think we will soon engineer the "perfect battery" to power electric cars that will go for long distances without re-charging. Elon Musk, CEO of Tesla, is focused on this accomplishment, as are other corporations. The applications will go way beyond powering vehicles and will enable the effective storage of energy for solar, wind, and wave technologies, making all of them more viable. Solar panels have been installed throughout the world in recent years. Australia is nearing an "all solar" solution. Here in the U.S., the utility companies have varied in their response to this. Some have been cooperative and others are charging large fees just to connect to the grid. These are issues that must be resolved.

This is an exciting era! The looming question is whether or not our government and industries will move out of the dark ages by continuing to support fossil fuels or end that age forever.

The choice is ours!

Chapter 7

● ● ●

Environmental Choices

❖ The Analyst

We have only one planet and cannot take any more risks or wait for action. Yet most environmental choices are based on short-term economics, ideology, and an inadequate sense of urgency at the highest level of decision making.

Technology has created the energy systems that have had a direct impact on our environment, and only technology can provide a solution. We will not dwell on the issues of climate deniers; we need to relentlessly move ahead on the solutions to environmental challenges. We cannot fix the environment after it is broken.

Trends, challenges, actions, opportunities

* In the United States, there is an inexplicable lack of, let us call it "excitement," about environmental threats. We certainly have many organizations that have been working for years on environmental concerns. But too many people have beliefs that fall under the category, "I'll believe it when I see it." The reality is that we are seeing it every day, but intermittently and in small doses. An

unusually mild winter, or rainy season, or other evidence of changing patterns that is too easily explained away as the vagaries of nature. Spoiler alert: when you can clearly see it, it will be too late. And if you do look, there is plenty of visible evidence: shrinking glaciers and polar ice caps, increasing frequency and intensity of large storms, and the suitability for some crops expanding their range to previously acceptable climates.

* In our own travels around the world we find greater awareness and concern about climatic changes than we do in the U.S. From Argentina to Italy, people are aware of the changes in growing seasons and geographic suitability for specific crops. People in Europe are not waiting for oranges to sprout in Switzerland, they are taking actions!

* Climate change deniers will be out of favor within the next three to five years. The unlikely hero may be the energy companies themselves. As political views change and evidence becomes more demanding, the global energy companies will do the literal turn-on-a-dime because they do not want to miss a single opportunity to convert their business to the energies of the future. We accept that energy companies can't just close oilfields and invest in alternative energies without a long-term plan, and obviously the costs of such a business changeover are vast. But they are intentionally and almost cruelly delaying the necessary efforts. The problem the energy and technology sectors will encounter is that their timing may be a misjudgment, and will find that their efforts may be too little, too late. Whatever the current cost to change policies and systems that affect the environment, it will cost multiples of that in the very near future. But this is typical corporate spreadsheet shortsightedness.

* We do not mean to be humorous, but accelerated and aggressive efforts to address environmental/climate threats will require someone with Al Gore's commitment but with an MTV personality. The financial markets have become entertainment through

creative media and high energy individuals. Environmental shifts will require similar creative and engaging communications to mobilize people who, in turn, will demand a political and business change of heart.

We are truly at or near the tipping point of unalterable changes in our environment that will determine the quality of life far into the future.

• • •

❖ The Astrologer

Scary Stuff

Since the publication of SILENT SPRING (Rachel Carson, 1962), *most of us have been witnessing both the debates about and the effects of human- generated pollution and global climate change. Most scientists believe this is caused by the proliferation of greenhouse gasses released into the atmosphere since the Industrial Revolution began in earnest in the 1800s. It was recently reported in multiple science and government publications that 2016 presented us with the hottest mean global temperature ever recorded. The recent 2017 report from the National Oceanic and Atmospheric Association (NOAA) reveals that the earth now has the highest concentration of CO2 in the air in 800,000 years!*

Glaciers are melting on mountains all over the world, in Antarctica, Alaska, and Greenland, and in the Himalayans, the Andes, the Sierra and Rocky Mountains, with the effect of diminishing inland supplies of fresh water and emptying glacier fresh water melt into the world's oceans. This fresh water is altering the salt content and disrupting the chemistry that supports the most important "thermohalent" currents like the Gulf Stream. For centuries, these warming currents are what have supported warm temperatures in Europe and the U.S., enabling the lengthy warm seasons for the growing of crops. Ironically, a similar melting and warming during the Middle Ages produced an agricultural prosperity, followed by the famous Mini Ice Age.

New "hot spots" in the oceans are creating "dead zones" that have exterminated life there. Oceanographers have instructed us that this phenomenon is known to contribute to the increased size of hurricanes. Huge typhoons have hit the Philippines, Japan, Indonesia, and Malaysia in recent years. We have recently witnessed the giant hurricanes Katrina, Sandy, Harvey, Irma, and Maria that hit the U.S. and its territories and broke all records in their intensity and destruction. Great coral reefs that form the basis of life in the oceans are dying. Many species of fish have already gone extinct. The earthquake and tsunami that destroyed the integrity of Japan's Fukushima nuclear plant brought about radioactive leaks into the Pacific Ocean that have shown up on the west coast of the U.S. from Alaska to Northern California. Radioactive remnants of all the atomic bomb explosions set off since the 1940s are circulating in the earth's atmosphere. This has led scientists to label our time as the Anthropocene era (distinct from the Holocene era, which began when glaciers retreated 11,700 years ago).

In the article, "A History in Layers," (*Scientific American*, Sept 2017, p.36), Professor Jan Zalasiewic published a graph listing chemical and industrial elements humans have deposited in and around the earth in massive amounts that include plastic (polymers), concrete, black carbon, plutonium 239 and 240, carbon dioxide, methane, and nitrous oxide. The author points out: "Our mines and boreholes penetrate several kilometers into the ground, so deep that these traces permanently scar the planet. The towns and cityscapes that have made over the earth's surface are also mirrored in subsurface foundations, pipelines, and subway systems."

In the same issue of *Scientific American* in the article, "How Will Climate Change Us," author Katie Peek writes: "An estimated 10 billion people will inhabit that warmer world. Some will become climate refugees, moving away from areas where unbearable temperatures are the norm and where rising water has claimed homes. In most cases, however, policy experts foresee relatively small movement within a country's borders. Most people and communities, cities and nations will adapt in place. We have highlighted roughly a dozen hotspots where climate change will disrupt humanity's living conditions and livelihoods, along with the strategies those communities are adopting to prepare for such a future." The parts of the world listed as the most threatened are: Newtok, Alaska, Tuvalu, Florida, the western U.S., Brazil, Lagos, Nigeria, Pakistan, Southern Africa, the Middle East, Southeast Asia, and Melbourne, Australia. I would advise you to read and study the article and the magazine in its entirety. This special issue is a treasure trove of information that may inform you and guide your decisions.

The advent of modern "industrialized farming" along with "relaxed" government monitoring has allowed massive usage of weed killers and insecticides sprayed on crops that both humans and animals are ingesting. The famous and controversial genetically- modified organisms (GMOs) are crops that were developed to survive these chemicals. This deregulatory trend has also resulted in the use of antibiotics and hormones in farm animals, designed to increase their weight and increase corporate profits. Some say that the result is obesity in the modern human population and a surge of antibiotic-resistant bacteria. Others believe that there is evidence to support that these chemicals may be behind bees and other pollinators becoming diseased and threatened with extinction. These same chemicals and massive amounts of petroleum-based fertilizers are also flowing into our oceans and inland aquifers. The article by Peek referenced above goes on to say: "We are also killing so many species that in another century or two the planet's biodiversity could take as catastrophic a hit as the one that happened when the dinosaurs disappeared." We might say that the famous human "footprint" has become the claw print of a million "Godzillas"!

The Unexpected

Surveying this landscape of seeming despair, the trends would appear to be marching us into a very dark future. I have a different take on all this, and that is, as an astrologer who looks hopefully ahead to the messages from planetary movements. With the coming **conjunction of Jupiter and Saturn in Aquarius** in 2020 and **Pluto going into Aquarius** in 2024 – 2044, I see our future from a different perspective. **Aquarius** is a constellational "sign" that is traditionally associated with cooling temperatures. As I was contemplating this, I wondered what "on earth" could happen in this cycle that has nothing to do with human-induced climate change.

One of the possibilities that came to mind was a possible extended Maunder Minimum, a long cycle of the "dying down" of storms and flares on the sun that has, in the past, resulted in a global cooling. This phenomenon occurred in the mid-1600s into the early 1700s and re-sulted in what is now known as the Mini Ice Age. An event like this could give us a reprieve and a period in which human civilization could invent its way out of the crisis. As the theory of synchronicity would suggest, a friend of mine emailed me an article, "Winter is Coming: Scientist Says Sun Will Nod Off in 15 Years," (Huffington Post, July 13, 2015). This was originally posted by Matt Berrical on the Van Winkles blog. Berrical reported: "Professor Vlentina Zharkova of Northumbria University presented the frigid findings at the National Astronomy Meeting in Llandudno, Wales. Modern technology has made us able to predict solar cycles with much greater accuracy and Zharkova's model predicts that solar activity will drop by more than half between 2030 and 2040." Berrical also reports: "The Maunder Minimum is the title given to period of time when sunspots are rare. It last occurred between 1645 and 1715, when roughly 50 sunspots were recorded as opposed to the standard 40,000. That time was marked by brutal river-freezing temperatures in Europe and North America."

Another part of this story involving the Mini Ice Age is that we know this period, as I stated earlier, as preceded by a lengthy global warming period in the Middle Ages helped produce viable crops in more northern locales. Thus, the melting of glaciers, similar to our present period, caused a de-salinization of water in the North Atlantic, as mentioned above. This chemical change in the Atlantic Ocean disrupted the important "thermo-halent" currents such as the Gulf Stream that historically have warmed Europe and North America, producing mild temperatures and enabling the growing of crops. We already know that the Gulf Stream is slowing down significantly at this point in time, another factor that would suggest a cooling cycle. What we do not know is the effect of this cooling cycle on a planet encased in greenhouse gases that have been deposited there since the mid-1800s. This is part of the uncertainty that lies ahead. The story has yet to be written.

Albert Einstein once said: "Either nothing is a miracle or everything is a miracle." I choose to believe we can tap into miracles!

Solutions

The most impressive book I have sourced on the environment is: *Drawdown: The Most Comprehensive Plan Ever Proposed to Reverse Global Warming*, edited by Paul Hawken (2017), which I referenced in my chapter on energy. This is a veritable encyclopedia of information containing solutions to reverse global warming, innovate and create new clean sources of energy, and create sustainable healthy economies around the world. I would suggest your taking the time to study what the leading experts in their various fields report in this book.

I will not attempt to include everything in this book which you may read for yourselves. However, the **Aquarian Age** on the horizon points to the possibilities involving breakthrough technologies that are the "keys to the kingdom" to a clean safe planet. Alongside solar, wind, wave, and geothermal energy, I believe an enormous solution is at hand, which I have been following for the past five years. I referred to this solution in the previous chapter on energy - Nuclear Fusion. In the chapter, "Hydrogen Boron Fusion," in the book, *Drawdown...*, *(p. 194)*, Hawken states: "Renewable energy, however, is variable and utilities want a steady source of energy that does not turn off. To that end, scientists and engineers have been pursuing the Holy Grail of physics since the 1930s - a clean, virtually unlimited source of energy that would take the world beyond the age of coal, gas, and oil, and power it for millennia into the future. Accomplishing star power would generate 'an inflection point in human history,' In the article, "2045: The Year Man Becomes Immortal" (*Time*, Feb 11, 2011) Lev Grossman declared: "an 'energy singularity' that would spell the end of fossil fuels." Many scientists hypothesize that this invention could be as great as the discovery of the wheel and could be the most important breakthrough in modern history.

Drawdown… also addresses how we may raise and consume healthy, environmentally sustainable food systems such as eating a plant-rich diet, farmland restoration, reduced food waste, regenerative agriculture, composting, and other technologies that require our attention and commitment. It contains valuable information about recycling, land use, transport, buildings, and cities. It presents an important chapter about women and girls with respect to small loans to women entrepreneurs, family planning, and the education of girls, especially in developing nations. The enormous growth of human populations on the planet, moving toward eight to nine billion, mostly in the poorest nations with the most frequent famines, could be modified by empowering women. These suggestions also contain information on recycling and cleaning up the deadly pollution we have deposited on land and in the world's oceans.

Another significant solution to the problem of the human ecological footprint lies in architecture and innovations in building construction. In my first book, *What Next? A Survival Guide to the 21ˢᵗ Century, (2007)* a chapter was written by solar architect, Donna Musial, with instructions about how to build an energy-efficient solar home. In recent years, so-called "passive" buildings have been built that are so effectively insulated that they need no central heat. This kind of architecture has been implemented in eco-villages throughout the world and is being lived in at the present time. Germany is one of the leaders in constructing these buildings, both for private homes and public buildings. Here in Ithaca, New

York, where I live, an eco-village has been constructed of this nature that has about one hundred units.

What is exciting to me is that many events are already taking place throughout the planet; the "magic" is already here; the genius is being implemented; the passion is alive and lives among us!

The choice is ours!

Chapter 8

• • •

Human Consciousness Philosophies, Beliefs, Choices and Transformation

❖ The Analyst

> *"We are what we think. All that we*
> *are arises with our thoughts.*
> *With our thoughts, we make the world."*

BUDDHA

We as individuals really do have the ultimate and decisive choice, but are we making the best of this gift? We can choose what we want, choose what we believe, or let someone choose for us.

We can talk about threats based on economics, technology, and all the other issues we have presented, but everyone is the result of what we believe individually and collectively. And it is obvious that we do not all have the same ideas, values, expectations, sense of responsibility, morality, and behaviors. And if we all have different beliefs, is it possible to agree on issues that are common to all of us — our way of life in the

United States and possibly our survival around the world? It might be possible, but it will not be easy, and we are far from achieving this common state of humanity.

The problem regarding our extinction/evolution issues is that people in the United States and across the world will not change their belief systems in any meaningful way, anytime soon, that can drive the efforts to solve the challenges we have presented.

We are making philosophical progress, however slowly, and the best we can do short-term is to be supremely pragmatic —to identify and present the critical challenges in a way that supersedes specific beliefs, secular or religious.

The concept of our thoughts and beliefs and how they can become a reality is one of the oldest interests of philosophers.

"Watch your thoughts, for they become words.
Watch your words, for they become actions.
Watch your actions, for they become habits.
Watch your habits, for they become character.
Watch your character, for it becomes your destiny."

LAO TZU

"Keep in mind this basic axiom—if all that now
exists was once imagined, then what you want to exist
for you in the future must now be imagined."

WAYNE W. DYER

"The world as we have created it is a process of our thinking.
It cannot be changed without changing our thinking."

ALBERT EINSTEIN

For this brief discussion we will use the term, beliefs, to encompass all religions, philosophies, ideologies, and any other systematic and widespread way of thinking.

Trends, challenges, actions, opportunities

* Of all the major areas of progress humans have made over the last several thousand years, the one aspect that seems to lag all others is our disparate and often conflicting belief systems. Today, in 2017, there seems to be as many religious and cultural conflicts around the world as can be imagined throughout history. There is no shortage of people and leaders actively seeking to promote greater divisiveness. The status of "beliefs" today I classify in three types:

  1. **Disillusionment with established beliefs.** These are seen as impractical, contradictory to other evidence, hypocritical in practice, have not progressed with the state of our general education, and perhaps, most important, are no longer providing satisfactory meaning or some type of spiritual fulfillment.

  2. **An apparent increase in the divergence of a commonality of beliefs.** These beliefs can be religious, cultural, social, ethnic, demographic, geographic, and biological. Are people around the world today becoming more confrontational and prejudiced? Or is this apparent divergence actually the last major resistance to belief systems that are no longer sufficient for our way of life? Are the conflicts in the news every day actually the very loud, frightened, and angry noise of the people who have not learned or been taught that the world is changing, and should change, and will change in beneficial ways? Part of the fear and frustration is tied to the many entities who want to remain in control of their positions and ideology and/or profit from the exploitation of the belief crisis.

3. **Hope for the future.** There is a measurble and increasing effort among many people for a belief practice or philosophy that makes sense based on what we know today scientifically by observation and is relevant and usable in our everyday life. I know this is happening because I have made the transition myself and have met other people with similar interests, but have been unable to find the spiritual home in current belief practices and institutions.

Over the past few years I have become involved in spirituality, metaphysics, started a blog, am writing a separate book, and have started "Meetups" about these topics.

The fundamental philosophical and metaphysical issue is whether individuals see themselves as part of a greater collective consciousness, existence, or as an individual entity exercising totally free will and independent from all other people. Are you part of something greater or are you alone and on your own? And how does your perception of this connection influence your choices?

Seeking a connection and evolving collectively is a distinctly human trait. Our immediate goal is not to extinguish ourselves before we have realized a greater goal.

From all recorded history, humans have an innate need to wonder about their existence and everything they see on the earth and in the skies above. This spiritual seeking seems to be in our DNA.

In the context of our extinction/evolution challenges, beliefs about laws, values, etc., are an integral part of our intellect. Humans have been very good at creating entire religious doctrines which have a fundamental concept of "doing good." It is also evident from our history and behavior that humans are not sufficiently evolved to practice uniform "doing good" and uniting people for the common good. We certainly do not practice what we preach, but perhaps we preach just to feel good. I would suggest that doing good will feel even better.

The immediate and divisive nature of our philosophical beliefs will take generations to resolve, but we need to build on the current reawakening. **Several trends and opportunities are evident, with one unlikely potential savior.**

* The information revolution enables everyone to be aware of alternative beliefs, political and economic systems, and every topic imaginable. Communications platforms will continue to be the enabler of more familiarity with other people which is necessary for creating comfort and tolerance of diversity. As noted earlier, we envision new information intelligence technologies that will minimize the level of intentional harmful communications that foster conflicts rather than peace.

* Over the last 20 years we have seen a reawakening of interest in spirituality, our place in the collective consciousness, and the pursuit of finding meaning and understanding of both "who we are" and "what we are supposed to do." Young people today are less dogmatic and with more secular beliefs and tolerance of our differences. We are just at the beginning of the resurgence in philosophical consciousness and the principles we follow individually and collectively will have a direct influence on the types of choices we make for each of the critical threats.

* "Follow the money" is a valid indicator of optimism. The sales of books, videos, seminars, retreats, and many other commercialized programs for personal empowerment, spiritual seeking, metaphysics, and religious offshoots is a booming industry in the U.S. and other developed countries. This renaissance of spirituality is relatively new, so there is a high level of charlatanism that can't be avoided. But my own work in metaphysics and ways to connect universal principles with practical applications convinces me that we humans still have the spark of greater good principles.

* We have a marked deficiency of quality leadership. The growing recognition and interest in spiritual values must be nurtured and

there must be leadership in a new reawakening — and this leadership is lacking. Religious philosophies must be, or in some way, incorporate more secular guidance. Organized religion today is unable to resolve our multiple conflicts and extinction/evolution challenges. Doctrines certainly need organization and rules, but if they also still include punitive elements, rejection of alternatives beliefs, and any teaching that promotes differences rather than inclusiveness will not survive nor will they help us solve our problems.

"One of the main functions of organized religion is to protect people against a direct experience of God."

C.G. JUNG

* Participation in traditional religions will continue to decline slowly. There is an opportunity for some of the existing religious movements, e.g., the mega-churches, to evolve their doctrines to be more focused on the evolution/extinction issues and to focus on practices that are earth-friendly and economically enlightened.

* Americans may be getting less religious, but feelings of spirituality are on the rise. Michael Masci and Michael Lipka of the Pew Research Center indicate that Americans are getting more *"spiritual but not religious."* This phrase has become widely used in recent years by some Americans who are trying to describe their religious identity. While the Pew Research Center does not categorize survey respondents in such a way, our surveys do find that the U.S. public overall appears to be growing a bit less religious, but also somewhat more spiritual.

* The unlikely savior from extinction/environmental challenges is to be found in commercial interests. Despite our critique of economic and political systems, they still are the most capable and adept at modifying and/or creating belief, desires, expectations, and satisfaction that can meet our challenges and serve the greater good. Every threat that we face offers a commercial/economic opportunity for current businesses and new entrepreneurs. If there is leadership, the will, and a profit to be made, there is more than adequate creativity and technology to help the shift to a new greater good psychology.

* One simple, yet one-in-a-million requirement is needed, at least in the short-term. Breakout leadership that recognizes the commercial opportunities of our survival and spiritual interests is needed, but leadership that also has genuine sincerity and, yes, call it charisma, theatrics, or entertainment skills that are necessary to get attention and change the minds that make the choices for beneficial change.

* If commercial leadership can lead a change in beliefs, attitudes, and economic actions for the greater good, over time these processes will become institutionalized in every aspect of our lives and will become the norm rather than elusive ideals.

• • •

❖ The Astrologer

Really Far Out

"I've loved the stars too fondly to be fearful of the night."

GALILEO GALILEI

As an astrologer, it has been my choice to experience my life and the lives of others as connected to nature, each other, and the observable universe. I see my journey and the journeys of human cultures and civilizations expressed through cycles that coincide with planetary movements through the starry constellations. Just as the seasons come and go, the earth moves through these great constellations in the sky, nations are born, rise, mature, and fall within the framework we refer to as time. The notion of a quantum reality with multi-verses in which we choose to look at a particle that exists within an infinity of universes is both interesting and appealing to me. Another notion that is appealing is that that there is no subjective or objective reality, there is just reality!

Articles and books are being written about a revolutionary idea that physicists have been discussing and examining in recent years. Interestingly, it was first introduced to me in one of my favorite sources, the inspiring Seth books by Jane Roberts (1963-1984). In two books, *Seth Speaks* (1972), and *The Nature of Personal Reality (1974)*, this revolutionary concept is that reality, or "All That Is" is consciousness itself! This theory hypothesizes that a "conscious" universe may be experiencing itself in an infinite number of possible or probable ways and that includes each one of us. This would lead us to the ultimate "choice" - accessing multiple universes with multiple possible selves making different decisions and choices beyond time itself and that our whole notion of "time" may be an error in judgment!

All this would lead us to the possibility that we may enter and exit our lives or "formats" but we never "die." It also echoes the axiom that matter is "neither created nor destroyed," it simply and endlessly changes its form, framework, or expression. What is being theorized in physics today recalls the ideas of reincarnation and karma from ancient Hinduism and modern Buddhism - that the core divine consciousness moves and cycles through all its possible evolutionary lifetimes living on into eternity. It reminds us of the promise of Christian theology that we may all have "eternal life." It would recall the religions of numerous native societies here in America and throughout the world who respected nature as having "divine" attributes linked by an eternal web of life. It inspires me to think. What could we do if we did not fear death?

Societal Advancement

Planetary occurrences and reoccurrences seem to point to an opportunity for humanity to advance from limited, local "predator/prey societies" and childish self-absorbed people-particles to a sharing, intelligent, mutually respectful social organization that would exist in concert with nature, respect individual creativity and innovation, and live within civil societies that stress negotiation and cooperation with one another. In addition, this society would admire individual innovation and respect differing opinions within the commons. Intelligent debate would replace intolerance and violence. Religious dogma would be replaced by the mutual insights held in common that are often shared by the original founders of these faiths.

Similar astrological patterns may "recycle" economic, political, technological, and even religious themes, but history never quite repeats itself; it becomes part of a larger spiral of consciousness growth. This happens if we, as humans, recognize that there is always "more to it" than the history behind it. Democracy in ancient Greece and the issuing of the Magna Carta in England both preceded the time of the American Revolution. The ideals repeated themselves, but there was a broader application of a rule of law, the notion of a Republic, and power to "the people" that would not have happened without the previous historic developments. Democracy and a parliamentary system of government will not work with officials whose personal development is infantile and selfish, whose interests are solely limited to their accumulation of personal wealth and power, and who are busy fighting each other at every turn until their accomplishments are Net Zero!

What Happened?

The tragedy of our recent history lies in grand and impressive technological development alongside a seeming lack of psychological and spiritual development; our return repetitively to murderous tribal wars, deliberate isolation and destruction; and a predator/prey "separatist" way of life whose inherent belief is that we must kill or enslave each other and grab territory in order to survive. The human notion that we have "ascendency" over nature has disconnected us from nature, the world, and each other leading to a sense that we are "entitled" to "commodify," kill, damage, and ravage everything around us. The fear of death lies at the bottom of the human psyche, for good reason. The form we inhabit instinctively seeks to preserve itself. However, if we could just begin to conceive ourselves as part and particle of each other, co-habiting a conscious system of universes, and whose finest expression could be one of cooperation, communication, and creativity, we could totally transform our very existence, past, present, and future. We could lay claim to the inspiring universal consciousness in which we all live.

Those who carried the light...

Great philosophers such as Plato, Socrates, Aristotle, Lao Tzu, Gautama Buddha, Moses, Jesus Christ, and many others have offered insights that we have studied, admired, and even worshiped but frequently failed to either practice or comprehend. I often contemplate the 20th century social and political idealists: Gandhi, King, and Mandala with their selfless devotion to peace, racial harmony, equality of opportunity, and how their societies imprisoned or assassinated them. India, after Mohandas Gandhi's great peaceful revolution for India's independence from Great Britain, fought a civil war between Hindus and Muslims resulting in Pakistan splitting into a separate nation that is still in an ongoing conflict with India. Both are armed with nuclear weapons. Gandhi was assassinated. Martin Luther King, Jr. launched arguably the greatest civil rights movement in U.S. history for equal respect and opportunity for all citizens regardless of race or social standing. He was assassinated. We have made very little progress today, seemingly moving backward, with greater disparities of the races in education, wealth, and respect for each other. Nelson Mandala heroically spent 27 years in solitary confinement in prison to rid South Africa of apartheid, and led his nation to embrace equality of opportunity and citizenship for all races, but the region is still far from anything that resembles "equal opportunity." Mandala stands out in that he "forgave" those who imprisoned him. There are many millions of others who are less visible and less famous, who grasp the principles of love, forgiveness, and are taking a firm stand for all of humanity, even at their own peril. Do we wish to be in this company?

"Time present and time past
Are both perhaps present in time future
And time future contained in time past.
If all time is eternally present
All time is unredeemable.
What might have been is an abstraction
Remaining a perpetual possibility
Only in a world of speculation
What might have been and what has been
Point to one end which is always present."

(*"Burnt Norton" by T.S. Elliott*)

Extinction or Evolution?

The damage human societies have done to the earth, our home, our miraculous complex biological system that gave birth to us, has reached such a point that we may have initiated our own extinction. We also have access to information, knowledge, and resources we never had before in all of history. Humans are developing the ability to travel to other planets and even become "colonists" on new earths. Do we wish to take our destructive behavior elsewhere to do it all over again? I do not believe this will happen until we solve the problems we have created here. Each and every one of us needs to make a choice whether or not to reach deeply within ourselves to see and know what we really are. It will take monumental courage and resolve to move along this road less traveled. We may all need to link hearts and minds to light the way. We could devise a "Hell on Earth" or initiate an "Evolving Paradise."

I believe that humanity is truly at the threshold of making a collective decision. As William Shakespeare darkly whispered through his character, Hamlet, "To be or not to be - that is the question."

The choice is ours!

Chapter 9

●　●　●

Practical Realities We Need to Face Choices We Need to Make

❖ The Analyst

These are the two key words to me: practical and reality. We have many high-level challenges that have converged. Individually they are serious issues, but collectively they can quickly evolve to irreversible harm to all of us.

I think the next ten years are the last time we will have to take substantive actions to reverse, stop, and remedy the most destructive trajectories in our economy, environment, and way of life.

Every facet of society is involved. While it is easy to categorize by sectors and constituencies, the practical reality is that they are all connected. They are as follows:

* Consumer involvement.
* Business objectives.
* Investment decisions.
* Technology priorities.
* Environmental security.
* Spiritual renaissance.

The business executive who makes an economic decision today is a consumer of cars, refrigerators, food, and books. A high-level financial executive making nanosecond trades has a 30-year mortgage and must pay his bills on time. The out-of-work industrial worker can write, talk, and vote, and is a valuable natural resource who just needs opportunity and education. The environmental activist is using the latest mobile technology to spread the word and raise the alarms.

The point is this – we are all entitled to our beliefs and ideologies, but we are all still subject to rules and choices made by others and the universal threats we discussed in this book.

We covered what we believe are the realities in this book, the specific issues, current trends, likely outcome if nothing is done, and suggestions for ways to change our choices and take actions.

The practical aspect is much more difficult. Our book is one of many voices trying to raise awareness and offer solutions for the many challenges. Similar efforts have been going on for decades, sometimes we seem to be making progress and then there are major periods of retreat as we experienced in 2016.

To me the practical reality is summarized in the wonderful statement that is an adaptation of many philosophers through the ages: *"Don't let the perfect be the enemy of the good."*

> Another widely-accepted interpretation of the phrase, *"The perfect is the enemy of the good,"* an aphorism or adaptation from the past, is that one might never complete a task if one has decided not to stop until it is perfect. Completing the project well is made impossible by striving to complete it perfectly. (*Wikipedia*)

And I like this one even better for today's challenges…

> Robert Watson-Watt, who developed early warning radar in Britain to counter the rapid growth of the Luftwaffe, propounded a "cult of the imperfect," which he described as: *"Give them the*

third best to go on with; the second best comes too late, the best never comes."(Wikipedia)

We have to make choices individually and collectively and waiting is not an option.

As individuals, we can do many things starting today:

* Get involved with existing organizations that share your concerns and ways to remedy the threats.
* Spend a little more time seeking and checking information that you need to make decisions.
* Vote for the right people. I do not agree with those who say it does not matter for whom you vote as long as you exercise your rights in a democracy and vote. It matters very much that you do both and that you vote for people with the progressive values to combat our major challenges.
* Make personal economic choices that essentially reward the providers of products and services that meet our goals and, in effect, boycott the businesses, politicians, and other leaders who are working for their interests and not ours.
* Find a spiritual, religious, or metaphysical practice that can help you personally. And if you are a member of an established religion, literally push for every day, real-life support that meets the fundamental tenets of all religions - to do good.
* Reverse one of the most insidious changes in our current trajectory of threats — the diminishment of education in general and liberal arts. In the United States, there is very little civic, philosophical, or intellectual education in public schools. And this is encouraged by extreme conservatism, religious fringe, and other powers that have just unimaginable motives for wanting to dumb down America. Unfortunately, it is working.

Collectively we need leadership that embraces the "greater good" policies and that has the personal ability, charisma, and skills to achieve the goals.

And probably my most heretical recommendation and wish — the real practical reality: fix our imminent challenges by making it popular and profitable to do so.

It is important that we have grassroots movements subsidized by credible media support for these necessary changes. Because no changes will ever occur unless it is clear to leaders that there is a philosophical and economic market for those changes. I am not being cynical, but political leaders, business leaders, and religious leaders already have the audience, organization, communication skills, and the connections to make a difference.

Current leaders can start, but we need to find and encourage the next generation of leaders who will begin a shift from largely economic motivations to the greater good objectives. Many of the people who should be the leaders now and in the future, are already out there, maybe they are activists in organizations, mayor of a progressive city, a high-tech entrepreneur, and others who already demonstrated skills that are needed but who also need the platform, economic justification, and, courage to take the next step.

The Analyst and the Astrologer - Next Steps

As soon as this book is published, some of the conversations will be at least somewhat out of date. The U.S. political scene may have changed, actual war may have started in North Korea or the Middle East, there will be another economic crisis, or something else that is bubbling below the surface. We believe the overall themes will remain a threat but the specifics that guide our actions will certainly evolve.

Thus, we will be starting a quarterly newsletter, *Our Choice – Extinction or Evolution*, as a supplement to cover the same issues in this book. Each addition will update the status and any other activity about our major challenges, identify any significant additions or changes, and do whatever else we can to support our own message.

Please check our website:

www.extinctionevolutionchoice.com

for more information about subscriptions to the quarterly newsletter beginning in January 2018.

$$\bullet \ \bullet \ \bullet$$

❖ The Astrologer

Moving through the threshold – The Age of Pisces to The Age of Aquarius

Transitions are never easy. As we witness economic and financial downturns, weather and environmental emergencies, and societal revolutions, we know that there will be those who will not survive. Many people with whom I have discussed these challenges have expressed the opinion that they do not want to live through all this. I am of the old-fashioned notion that I got from my parents and grandparents. This notion is: "Never, ever, ever give up"! We will all be "transitioning to the next world" eventually. Let's give it our best shot while we are still in this one!

Getting through the immediate crisis

On a very practical level, the first step may be to get out of debt. Have no mortgage or credit card balances, if possible. If you can own your home and your vehicle outright, this is a good thing! If it is financially possible, it could be helpful to own income-producing properties. Remember, the value of real estate is always local and requires research on your part as to the viability of this choice. At home, have a source of heat that is off the electric grid such as solar panels, a gas fireplace, or wood burning stove. Growing your own food organically in a container or in your back yard is a desirable option. Interestingly, there is currently a "tiny house" movement in which many young people are investing themselves. They buy or build a tiny house with a minimum and sustainable life-style, often with solar panels. Many of these units are on wheels and can be transported around the country to wherever there is employment. Often, this housing is inexpensive and requires no mortgage. Young people are finding out they can live simply, debt free, and unencumbered without a lot of "things."

As I have suggested in previous chapters, we all need to come face-to-face with global climate change, rising oceans, emerging deserts, and increasing catastrophic hurricanes. I think we are just beginning to grasp these realities in the U.S. following Hurricanes Harvey, Irma, and Maria. **I HAVE BEEN URGING PEOPLE TO CONSIDER MOVING INLAND TO PLACES OF ELEVATION WITH PLENTY OF FRESH WATER AND FARMLAND** since my first book, *What Next?: A Survival Guide to the 21st Century* (2007). The U.S. is fortunate in that we have a huge amount of viable land. We have the Great Lakes, the largest supply of inland fresh water in the world, except for the Amazon River Basin. Although our "empire" may be in a decline, new ways of life within the context of the Green Revolution are possible for us. We are blessed with a geography that can sustain life.

Another old-fashioned notion is to save and stash your cash. It will still be "good" for a while before digital currency takes over. A good practice is to store supplies of preserved food, potable water, and medical supplies in case of emergencies of any kind. Gold coins are another option as long as they are real currency. Some long-term financial investments could be: cyber security companies, water conservation and purification companies, and sustainable energy corporations. Technology stocks will continue to grow, but coming bear markets on Wall Street will bring these stocks down temporarily.

The Greater Vision

Most importantly, we need to recognize that we need to work together: friends, families, groups of various kinds. I noticed that during the recent mega-hurricanes that struck Texas, Florida, and Puerto Rico, thousands of people rallied their resources and assisted, rescued, and exhibited a concern and kindness for others that restored my faith in humanity.

Civilizations do not survive well with individuals marching alone in the wilderness with a gun, a match, and an ax. This is okay for a while for a few very young, very fit, and militarily trained individuals, but these people will have accidents, get sick, and get old. Friendly cities and neighborhoods who are respectful and tolerant of differences yet willing to work together imitates "nature" which is a highly effective INTERDEPENDENT matrix of species that sustains the miracle of life. We can dissent, disagree, and debate, but let us stop killing each other! We need to develop from "tribes" with chiefs and kings, to cooperative local communities in which all participate in their governance. Joining an eco-village, an environmental group, or organic farming and gardening cooperatives can contribute to the planet and to one another. Respect for each other needs to be restored and seen as a "survival" tactic.. Ironically, this requires that we take responsibility as individuals to innovate and create new economic and societal systems that minimize the old "evils."

Most of all, it will require of us a determination, a will to survive, and an overriding hope and passion that the future is worth it! Our children and grandchildren are awaiting our decision.

The choice is ours!

We hope you've enjoyed this book. If you'd like to continue to follow our work on astrology, metaphysics and extinction/evolution threats, please visit our websites.

Linda Schurman

http://www.soothesayer.com/

Richard Spitzer

Blog
http://www.universalprinciples1.com/

Macro Research
http://3imacroanalytics.com/

Appendix

A. Historic Definitive Astrological Placements

Pluto/Saturn conjunction in Libra Nov. 1982, Jupiter/Saturn conjunction in Taurus May 2000, Pluto/ Saturn opposition took place in Sagittarius and Gemini Sept. 2001, Saturn/Uranus square in Virgo and Pisces occurred in Oct. 2008 plus Pluto hit the Galactic Center at 28 degrees of Sagittarius, Pluto/Saturn square in Capricorn and Libra hit in Jan. 2010, Pluto/Uranus square in Capricorn and Aries occurred from March 2012 – Dec. 2015, Saturn reaches the Galactic Center April through November 2017, Uranus goes into Taurus May 2018 through Nov. 2018, back into Aries and into Taurus March 2019 through April 2026, Uranus enters Gemini July 2025 – 2033, Neptune transits in Pisces April 2011 – January 2026, Neptune enters Aries Jan. 2026 - 2039,   Pluto/Saturn conjunction occurs in Capricorn Jan. 2020, Jupiter/Saturn Conjunction takes place Aquarius Dec. 2020, Uranus transits Taurus May 2018 - 2025, Pluto transits Aquarius Jan. 2024 – 2044.

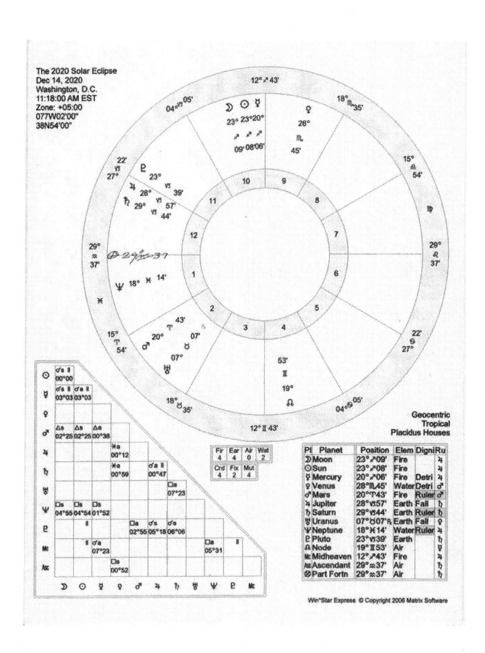

The 2020 Solar Eclipse
Dec 14, 2020
Washington, D.C.
11:18:00 AM EST
Zone: +05:00
077W02'00"
38N54'00"

Geocentric
Tropical
Placidus Houses

Fir	Ear	Air	Wat
4	4	0	2

Crd	Fix	Mut
4	2	4

Pl	Planet	Position	Elem	Digni	Ru
☽	Moon	23°♐09'	Fire		♃
☉	Sun	23°♐08'	Fire		♃
☿	Mercury	20°♐06'	Fire	Detri	♃
♀	Venus	28°♏45'	Water	Detri	♂
♂	Mars	20°♈43'	Fire	Ruler	♂
♃	Jupiter	28°♑57'	Earth	Fall	♄
♄	Saturn	29°♑44'	Earth	Ruler	♄
♅	Uranus	07°♉07'℞	Earth	Fall	♀
♆	Neptune	18°♓14'	Water	Ruler	♃
♇	Pluto	23°♑39'	Earth		♄
☊	Node	19°♊53'	Air		☿
Mc	Midheaven	12°♐43'	Fire		♃
Asc	Ascendant	29°♒37'	Air		♄
⊗	Part Fortn	29°♒37'	Air		♄

Win*Star Express © Copyright 2006 Matrix Software

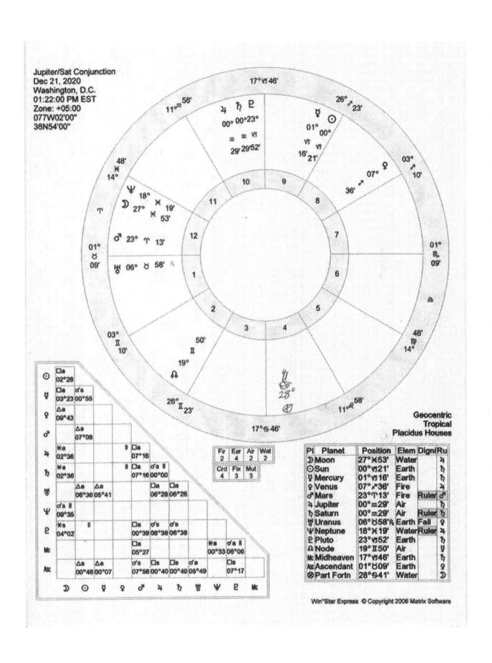

Jupiter/Sat Conjunction
Dec 21, 2020
Washington, D.C.
01:22:00 PM EST
Zone: +05:00
077W02'00"
38N54'00"

Geocentric
Tropical
Placidus Houses

Fir	Ear	Air	Wat
2	4	2	2

Crd	Fix	Mut
4	3	3

Pl	Planet	Position	Elem	Digni	Ru
☽	Moon	27°♓53'	Water		♃
☉	Sun	00°♑21'	Earth		♄
☿	Mercury	01°♑16'	Earth		♄
♀	Venus	07°♐36'	Fire		♃
♂	Mars	23°♈13'	Fire	Ruler	♂
♃	Jupiter	00°♒29'	Air		♄
♄	Saturn	00°♒29'	Air	Ruler	♄
♅	Uranus	06°♉58'R	Earth	Fall	♀
♆	Neptune	18°♓19'	Water	Ruler	♃
♇	Pluto	23°♑52'	Earth		♄
☊	Node	19°♊50'	Air		☿
Mc	Midheaven	17°♑46'	Earth		♄
Ac	Ascendant	01°♉09'	Earth		♀
⊗	Part Fortn	28°♋41'	Water		☽

Win*Star Express © Copyright 2006 Matrix Software

121

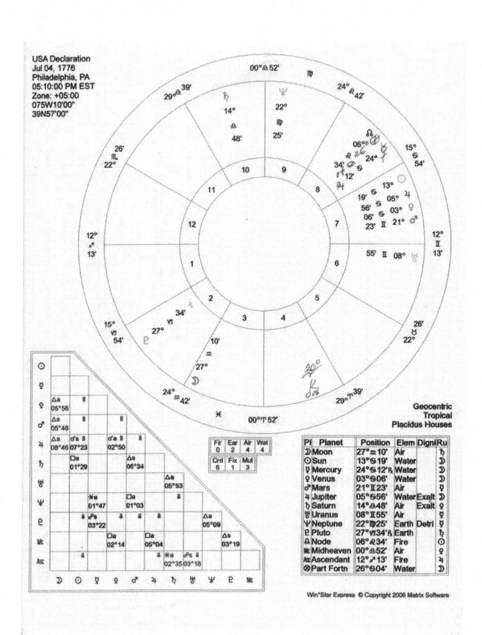

USA Declaration
Jul 04, 1776
Philadelphia, PA
05:10:00 PM EST
Zone: +05:00
075W10'00"
39N57'00"

Geocentric
Tropical
Placidus Houses

Fir	Ear	Air	Wat
0	2	4	4

Crd	Fix	Mut
6	1	3

Pl	Planet	Position	Elem	Digni	Ru
☽	Moon	27°≈10'	Air		♄
☉	Sun	13°♋19'	Water		☽
☿	Mercury	24°♋12'℞	Water		☽
♀	Venus	03°♋06'	Water		☽
♂	Mars	21°♊23'	Air		☿
♃	Jupiter	05°♋56'	Water	Exalt	☽
♄	Saturn	14°♎48'	Air	Exalt	♀
♅	Uranus	08°♊55'	Air		☿
♆	Neptune	22°♍25'	Earth	Detri	☿
♇	Pluto	27°♑34'℞	Earth		♄
☊	Node	06°♌34'	Fire		☉
Mc	Midheaven	00°♎52'	Air		♀
Asc	Ascendant	12°♐13'	Fire		♃
⊗	Part Fortn	26°♋04'	Water		☽

Win*Star Express © Copyright 2006 Matrix Software

122

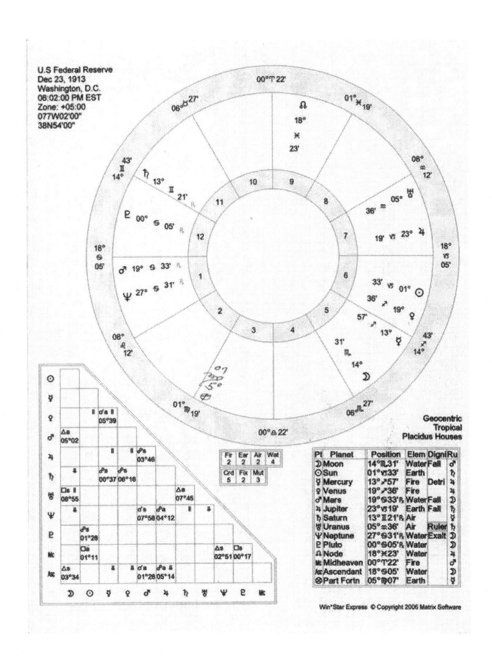

U.S Federal Reserve
Dec 23, 1913
Washington, D.C.
06:02:00 PM EST
Zone: +05:00
077W02'00"
38N54'00"

Geocentric
Tropical
Placidus Houses

Fir	Ear	Air	Wat
2	2	2	4
Crd	Fix	Mut	
5	2	3	

Pl	Planet	Position	Elem	Digni	Ru
☽	Moon	14°♏31'	Water	Fall	♂
☉	Sun	01°♑33'	Earth		♄
☿	Mercury	13°♐57'	Fire	Detri	♃
♀	Venus	19°♐36'	Fire		♃
♂	Mars	19°♋33'℞	Water	Fall	☽
♃	Jupiter	23°♑19'	Earth	Fall	♄
♄	Saturn	13°♊21'℞	Air		☿
♅	Uranus	05°♒36'	Air	Ruler	♄
♆	Neptune	27°♋31'℞	Water	Exalt	☽
♇	Pluto	00°♋05'℞	Water		☽
☊	Node	18°♓23'	Water		♃
⋆	Midheaven	00°♈22'	Fire		♂
As	Ascendant	18°♋05'	Water		☽
⊗	Part Fortn	05°♍07'	Earth		☿

Win*Star Express © Copyright 2006 Matrix Software

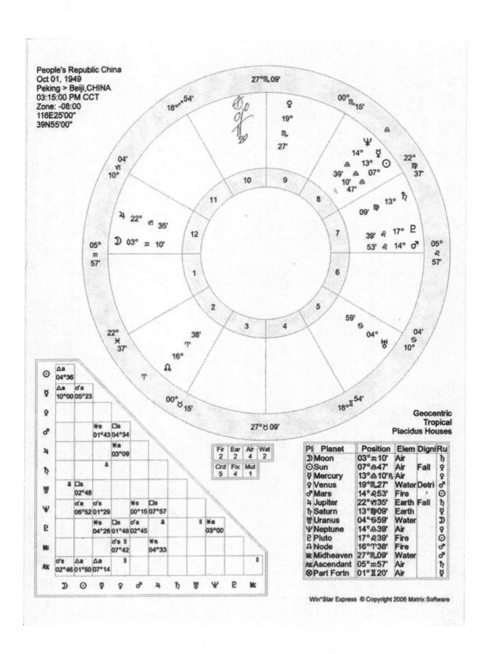

People's Republic China
Oct 01, 1949
Peking > Beiji,CHINA
03:15:00 PM CCT
Zone: -08:00
116E25'00"
39N55'00"

Geocentric
Tropical
Placidus Houses

Fir	Ear	Air	Wat
2	2	4	2

Crd	Fix	Mut
5	4	1

Pl	Planet	Position	Elem	Digni	Ru
☽	Moon	03°≈10'	Air		♄
☉	Sun	07°♎47'	Air	Fall	♀
☿	Mercury	13°♎10'℞	Air		♀
♀	Venus	19°♏27'	Water	Detri	♂
♂	Mars	14°♌53'	Fire		☉
♃	Jupiter	22°♑35'	Earth	Fall	♄
♄	Saturn	13°♍09'	Earth		☿
♅	Uranus	04°♋59'	Water		☽
♆	Neptune	14°♎39'	Air		♀
♇	Pluto	17°♌39'	Fire		☉
☊	Node	16°♈38'	Fire		♂
Mc	Midheaven	27°♏09'	Water		♂
Asc	Ascendant	05°≈57'	Air		♄
⊗	Part Fortn	01°♊20'	Air		☿

Win*Star Express © Copyright 2006 Matrix Software

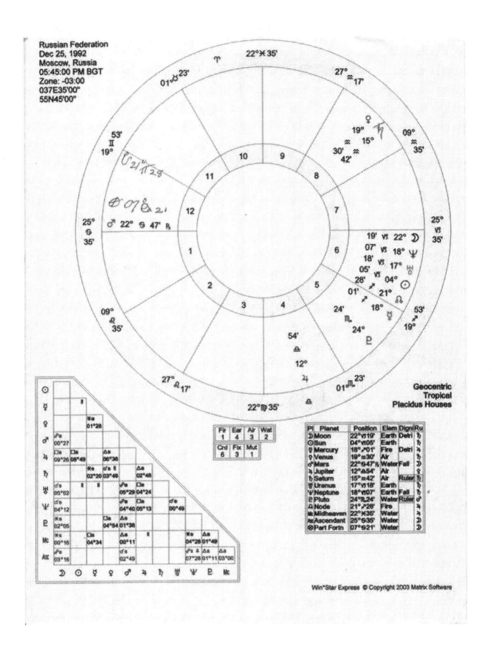

Russian Federation
Dec 25, 1992
Moscow, Russia
05:45:00 PM BGT
Zone: -03:00
037E35'00"
55N45'00"

Geocentric
Tropical
Placidus Houses

Fir	Ear	Air	Wat
1	4	3	2

Crd	Fix	Mut
6	3	1

Pl	Planet	Position	Elem	Digni	Ru
☽	Moon	22°♑19'	Earth	Detri	♄
☉	Sun	04°♑05'	Earth		♄
☿	Mercury	18°✶/01'	Fire	Detri	♃
♀	Venus	19°♒30'	Air		♄
♂	Mars	22°♋47'ℝ	Water	Fall	☽
♃	Jupiter	12°♌54'	Air		☉
♄	Saturn	15°♒42'	Air	Ruler	♄
♅	Uranus	17°♑18'	Earth		♄
♆	Neptune	18°♑07'	Earth	Fall	♄
♇	Pluto	24°♏24'	Water	Ruler	♂
☊	Node	21°♐28'	Fire		♃
Mc	Midheaven	22°✶35'	Water		♃
As	Ascendant	25°♋35'	Water		☽
⊕	Part Fortn	07°♋21'	Water		☽

Win*Star Express © Copyright 2003 Matrix Software

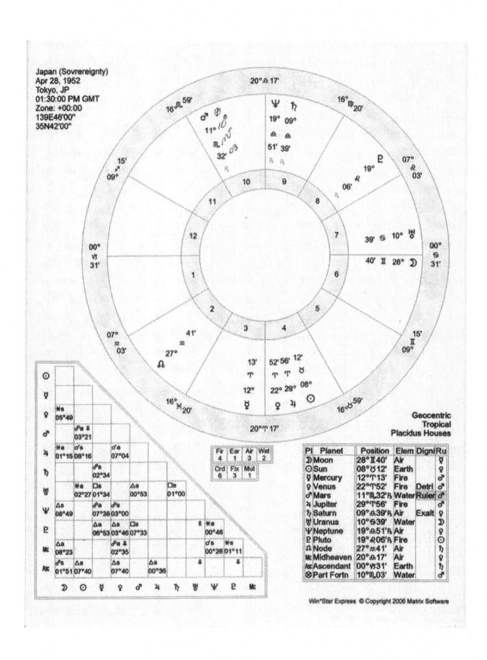

Japan (Sovrereignty)
Apr 28, 1952
Tokyo, JP
01:30:00 PM GMT
Zone: +00:00
139E46'00"
35N42'00"

Geocentric
Tropical
Placidus Houses

Fir	Ear	Air	Wat
4	1	3	2

Crd	Fix	Mut
6	3	1

Pl	Planet	Position	Elem	Digni	Ru
☽	Moon	28°Ⅱ40'	Air		☿
☉	Sun	08°♉12'	Earth		♀
☿	Mercury	12°♈13'	Fire		♂
♀	Venus	22°♈52'	Fire	Detri	♂
♂	Mars	11°♏32'℞	Water	Ruler	♂
♃	Jupiter	29°♈56'	Fire		♂
♄	Saturn	09°♎39'℞	Air	Exalt	♀
♅	Uranus	10°♋39'	Water		☽
♆	Neptune	19°♎51'℞	Air		♀
♇	Pluto	19°♌06'℞	Fire		☉
☊	Node	27°♈41'	Fire		♂
Ⓜ	Midheaven	20°♎17'	Air		♀
Asc	Ascendant	00°♑31'	Earth		♄
⊗	Part Fortn	10°♏03'	Water		♂

Win*Star Express © Copyright 2006 Matrix Software

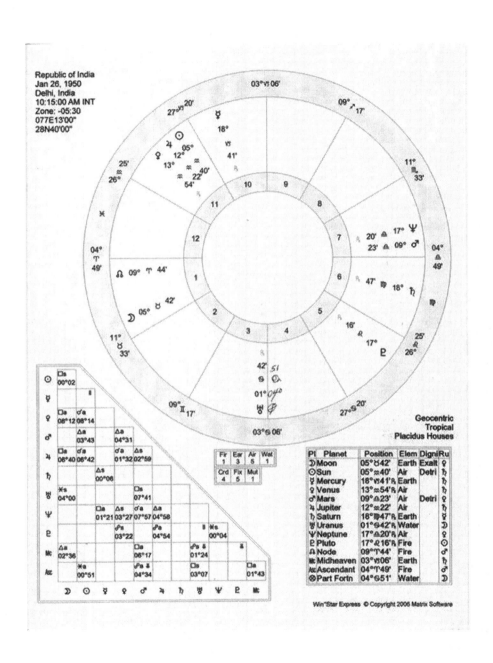

Republic of India
Jan 26, 1950
Delhi, India
10:15:00 AM INT
Zone: -05:30
077E13'00"
28N40'00"

Geocentric
Tropical
Placidus Houses

Fir	Ear	Air	Wat
1	3	5	1

Crd	Fix	Mut
4	5	1

Pl Planet	Position	Elem	Digni	Ru
☽ Moon	05°♉42'	Earth	Exalt	♀
☉ Sun	05°♒40'	Air	Detri	♄
☿ Mercury	18°♑41'℞	Earth		♄
♀ Venus	13°♒54'℞	Air		♄
♂ Mars	09°♎23'	Air	Detri	♀
♃ Jupiter	12°♒22'	Air		♄
♄ Saturn	18°♍47'℞	Earth		☿
♅ Uranus	01°♋42'℞	Water		☽
♆ Neptune	17°♎20'℞	Air		♀
♇ Pluto	17°♌16'℞	Fire		☉
☊ Node	09°♈44'	Fire		♂
Mc Midheaven	03°♑06'	Earth		♄
As Ascendant	04°♈49'	Fire		♂
⊕ Part Fortn	04°♋51'	Water		☽

Win*Star Express © Copyright 2006 Matrix Software

About the author

Economic and historical astrologer Linda Schurman has been publishing newsletters and astrological interpretations for over forty years. Her writings on social, economic, and environmental issues predicted the severity of the 2008 economic collapse.

The author of two previous books on astrological guidance and cyclical influences on economics, technology, social conditions, and politics, Schurman maintains a website at www.soothsayer.com.

Richard Spitzer has over forty years of experience designing research studies on topics at once diverse and interconnected, including future trends, communication influences, business, economics, and consumer behavior.

In 2004 Spitzer launched a business based on his new macrotrend analytics methodology based on text and predictive analytics. More information on Spitzer and his business may be found at www.3imacroanalytics.com.

70900654R10088

Made in the USA
San Bernardino, CA
08 March 2018